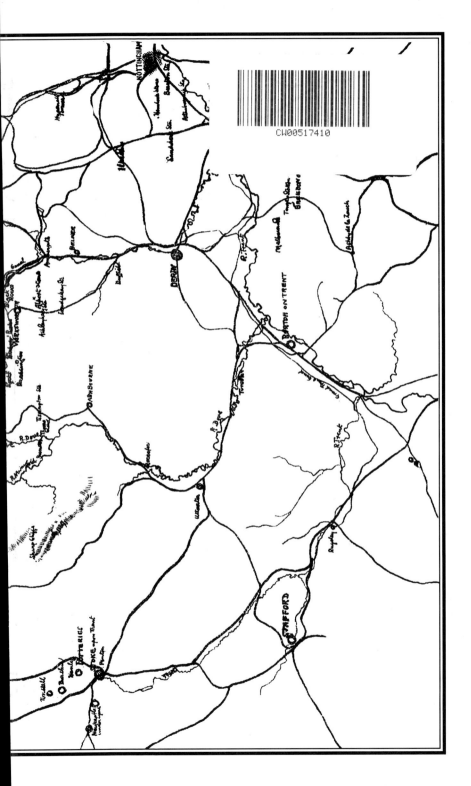

MOORS, CRAGS & CAVES
OF THE
HIGH PEAK
AND THE NEIGHBOURHOOD

ERNEST A. BAKER, M.A. (Lond)

Author of *A Descriptive Guide to the Best Fictions.*
Editor of *Half-forgotten Books.*

HALSGROVE

First published by John Haywood Ltd 1903
Second facsimile edition 2002
Introduction copyright © 2002 Roly Smith

ISBN 1 84114 171 2

British Library Cataloguing-in-Publication Data
A CIP record for this title is available from the British Library

HALSGROVE
Halsgrove House
Lower Moor Way
Tiverton, Devon EX16 6SS
T: 01884 243242
F: 01884 243325
sales@halsgrove.com
www.halsgrove.com

Printed and bound in Great Britain by
Bookcraft Ltd, Midsomer Norton

TO THE

Rev. DAVID MACDONALD, M.A., B.D.,

First President of the Kyndwr Club,

AND

Comrade of the Author on Many of the Rambles

and Scrambles Herein Commemorated

Photo by   G.A. Fowkes, Derby.

BRASSINGTON ROCKS – A FACE CLIMB.

INTRODUCTION

———

*M*OORS, *Crags and Caves of the High Peak and the Neighbourhood* was first published in 1903, and is widely-recognised as a classic account of early walking, climbing and caving in the Peak District. Indeed, it is one of the earliest books ever published in Britain about these esoteric, but now so popular, sports.

It recounts the exploits of the redoubtable Kyndwr Club, a group of Sheffield and Derby walkers and climbers which was founded in 1900 – coincidentally the same year as G.H.B. Ward's equally-famous Clarion Ramblers in Sheffield.

Dr. Ernest A. Baker led the Derby contingent of the Kyndwr Club, and *Moors, Crags and Caves* is his personal account of some of the club's most notable early expeditions, including many first ascents – and descents – of the Peak's crags and caves.

At the time, Baker was the Librarian at Derby's Midland Institute, and was later to become nationally-known as the author of the ten-volume *History of the English Novel*. His other outdoor books included *The Highlands with Rope and Rucksack* (1923) and *On Foot in the Highlands* (1932).

Baker's descriptive accounts in *Moors, Crags and Caves*, especially those of crossing the high, and at that time forbidden, moorlands, have rightly become classics in Peakland literature. Culled mostly from articles first published in the *Manchester Guardian*, the *Climbers' Club Journal*, *Wide World Magazine* and *The Field*, they describe the contemporary need for permits to walk on the vast moorlands of Kinder Scout, and his frequent encounters with gamekeepers en route.

Baker's work has often been criticised for being overtly egotistical, especially in his accounts of walking and climbing. He mentions none of his other companions by name, although they are known to have included the formidable J.W.Puttrell of Sheffield, who was generally acknowledged to be the leading rock climber of his day.

Writing in *High Peak, the history of walking and climbing in the Peak District* published in 1966, Eric Byne and Geoffrey Sutton complained that the reader of *Moors, Crags and Caves* was left with the impression that Baker was the leading light in every excursion, although this was far from the truth.

"He was the leading organiser of the Derby group and the chronicler of the club's activities, at both of which jobs he did outstandingly well; but he was never, as he gives the reader to understand, the leader in action. Contemporary testimony is unanimous in assigning this place to Puttrell."

An example of this are his accounts of his attempts on the fearsome 120-foot High Tor Gully at Matlock Bath, on which he admits failing twice and adds: "I will not predict that nobody will be found daring enough to clamber, with the aid of a rope, from one gigantic chockstone to the next, but the dark, cave-like aspect of the dismal place took from us any desire to attempt the feat." In the Kyndwr Club notes in the *Climbers' Club Journal* of 1903, he mentioned that members had been successful in climbing the gulley, but significantly refrained from giving their names. It had been led that year by Puttrell, and the new club president William Smithard, a founder member of the Derbyshire Footpaths Preservation Society, had written an account of this "splendid and enjoyable" climb, led with the "usual dash and courage" by Puttrell.

Disgusted by Baker's evident envy and jealousy, Smithard wrote a strong letter in defence of the climb, to which Baker apparently replied in "fiery" terms. A bitter controversy raged between the two in succeeding issues of the *Journal*, as it became plain, according to Byne and Sutton, that Baker was not prepared to recognise, at least in print, the climbing qualities and achievements of his friends. From that time on, the Kyndwr Club began to fall apart, and Smithard and others severed all connection with Baker and his Derby circle, aligning themselves with Puttrell's Sheffield group. Eventually, with Smithard now editing the club notes, Baker resigned and joined the Manchester-based Rucksack Club.

Baker and Puttrell had probably first met around 1898, because they were both founder members of the Climbers' Club which began in that year. Byne and Sutton suggest that they probably met on a climbing meet in the Matlock area, at a time when Baker was first becoming interested in Peakland moors and crags. His first rock climb was apparently the isolated Alport Stone near Wirksworth. He wrote an article on "Practice Scrambles in the Peak District" in the first *Climbers' Club Journal* and was later to describe many of the club's early outings on Kinder Scout, Bleaklow and the Eastern Edges in *Moors, Crags and Caves*.

The first signs of envy in Baker's manner became evident as early as 1900, after Puttrell had led the Stonnis Crack route at Cromford Black Rocks. He belittled Puttrell's performance, declaring that there was no point in climbing so riskily, and even claimed in print that there had been no confirmation of the "rumour" of the first ascent.

In June of the same year, the club met on Puttrell's home ground of Wharncliffe Rocks, and the competition between the two camps was evident as the party negotiated the "Monkey Jump" from the top of the Bass Rock. The Sheffielders accomplished the feat with the ease of familiarity, but Baker, as a contemporary verse described, hesitated.

He laughed at Baker's determined look
As the situation in he took.
He thought he would, then thought he wouldn't,
Believed he could and perhaps he couldn't,
Prepared to try, then sat to think,
And still he sat just on the brink.

Eventually, Baker was forced to accept an ignominious defeat.

Whatever his faults, Baker was without doubt a tireless campaigner for the rights of walkers and climbers to have free access to open moorland and mountain. According to Byne and Sutton, "His love of the high moors was very deep and sincere, and the efforts of owners and game-keepers to forbid access to them were a challenge to his passion for exploration. Puttrell and the others might be quite satisfied with the fun of trespassing, but not Baker."

He made himself a champion of rights-of-way and the right to roam, and was to remain keenly interested in the struggle for access throughout his life. As early as 1923 in his *The Highlands with Rope and Rucksack*, he complained: "The aim of the owners of the deer forests is to create a huge solitude first by removing such human population, then closing mountains and glens to the public. They have succeeded in doing this throughout a large proportion of ten counties; of 543 peaks obtaining the Munro Standard 3,000 feet above sea level, nearer 500 than 400 are situated in this forbidden land."

This was a title he referred to frequently, and in an article bearing the same heading in the *Ramblers' Manchester Federation Handbook* the following year about the regaining of these old freedoms in the Peak, he wrote: "These barren tracts never had the abundance of pasture where the com-moner could graze his beasts, or of woods and spinneys where he had the right to gather fireing; hence the claims to commonage were unimportant. Thus the moorlands remained waste lands out and out and nobody troubled much about them. So far as access was concerned, no let or hinderance was interposed by needless landowners."

Baker was a leading supporter of Annan Bryce's Access to Mountains Bill of 1908, complaining about the fact that there was then nowhere for a walker to stay on the ancient Scottish 50-mile cross-country right of way up Glen Affric and Glen Lichd. He also took a leading role in Phil Barnes's campaign which tried to salvage something from Creech Jones's severely emasculated Access to Mountains Act of 1939. This included speaking at a huge rally attended by 800 people in London, alongside Hugh Dalton MP and Stephen Morton, the RA activist from Sheffield.

The passing of the Countryside and Rights of Way Act in 2000, which will eventually give ramblers that long-cherished "right to roam" in designated open country, could be seen as a suitable memorial to Ernest Baker and his brave band of early Kyndwr Club trespassers.

Roly Smith, April 2002

PREFACE

———

The Author's thanks are due to the Editors of the *Manchester Guardian*, the *Climbers' Club Journal*, the *Wide World Magazine*, and the *Field*, for permission to reprint certain chapters of this volume; and to the Editors of the *Climbers' Club Journal* and the *Yorkshire Ramblers' Club Journal*, and other friends, for illustrations. Mr. H. Arnold Bemrose, F.G.S., kindly supplied two sections of caves, and Mr. James Porter drew the valuable plan of Bagshawe Cavern.

CONTENTS.

List of Illustrations.

MOORS, CRAGS, and CAVES of the High Peak

AND THE NEIGHBOURHOOD.

I.

WINTER DAYS ON KINDER SCOUT.

The time seems near, if it has not actually arrived, when the chastened sublimity of a moor, a sea, or a mountain will be all of nature that is absolutely in keeping with the moods of the more thinking among mankind.—The Return of the Native.

 A CHARACTERISTIC of Peak scenery endearing it to the hardy rambler is that it loses nothing of its peculiar glory in winter. Right in the centre of England, midway between Sheffield and Manchester, at the threshold of the world's most populous cluster of manufacturing towns, there lies this broad area of wild country, as lone and untamed as any south of Cheviot. Through the factory smoke and the steam we have glimpses, now and again, of the dark line of the edges. Even business is lightened a little by the knowledge that an hour or two might take us clean away, on to a heathery moor that wears the

same harsh, impassible face it wore when Britain was peopled by savages. Whether it be, as Thomas Hardy maintains so eloquently, that these austere landscapes, whose prophecy is as sombre as their history, are naturally in harmony with our modern pessimism, or that they exercise a tonic influence upon our pampered and jaded minds; or whether it be merely the physical sense of space and freedom, or the suggestions of the mysterious and the illimitable with which the shadowy expanses and the dark ravines sway the imagination as with the suggestiveness of poetry; true it is that the gloomy scenes which our grandfathers hated, draw us with a subtle and a powerful spell.

Winter is most in keeping with such scenery. Then the gaunt crags, bristling along the edges of the moorlands, loom through veils of cloud that transfigure and idealise; the withered heather is susceptible of all the tints flung upon it by the vagaries of the sunlight; and the tracts of coarse grass, embrowned and burnt red by frost, are changed through a hundred gradations of warm, rich colour. Winter, again, with storms and flooded cloughs, with deep snow-wreaths, ice-clad rocks, and bewildering mists, affords the incorrigible wanderer a little of the adventure for which he is ready to travel much farther afield.

Peakland scenery culminates in Kinder Scout, to which, by a confusion of ideas, the Ordnance Surveyors gave the name of a whole district. Unabashed by its flatness, they called it the Peak. In a number of places the Scout rises above the 2,000ft. level; it has the noblest crags, the biggest peat-moss, and the finest waterfall in the district. Its waters run to the eastern and western seas, the cloughs that penetrate to the heart of it are like mountain corries, with turbulent streams rushing to the dales. And Kinder Scout in

Photo by   *Richard Keene, Ltd., Derby.*

IN GRINDSBROOK CLOUGH, LOOKING TOWARDS THE EDGE.

winter is as wild a place as any mountain in England or Wales. To cross it is no less of an adventure than to cross Scawfell under like conditions, and the grandeur and novelty of the experience repay one quite as well.

My first ascent of the Scout was made years ago during a winter of memorable severity. For long weeks the deep drifts were sealed up with frost; many sheep and cattle perished; the wild things were, like the hares, slain in hundreds, or driven like the grouse to seek the abodes of man and pick up a living with the domestic fowls; lines were blocked, mail-carts snowed up, and several people were caught and overcome in the storms. Our party of four came to the new station at Edale, accoutred for the fray. Wild indeed was the scene that opened on us when we emerged from Totley Tunnel. The dales with their pine woods, black and gaunt, set against the snow-slopes; the dark crags high aloft, the " cornices " of snow along the ridges; and the dark-brown, heaving Derwent, swirling along sombrely below, altogether made a thoroughly highland picture. Most imposing was the lofty cirque immuring the head of Edale; Mam Tor, Lord's Seat, and Cowburn, rising up and up until their white slopes melted, with no visible line of contour, into the whiteness of the mist.

No sooner had we left the hamlet of Edale Chapel and the homestead at the foot of Grindsbrook Clough, than we found ourselves entering a very arctic world. A half-obliterated cart-road led through a spinney to the open moor. Down the middle of the deep, rugged clough ran the Grindsbrook, if it could be said to run when the springs were congealed, and all the cascades stricken into stalactites of greenish-blue ice. To right and left stretched long slopes of snow up to the clouds, the head of the clough was full of whirling mist that boded trouble, and hundreds of feet above our heads the sharp end of Ringing Rocher towered like a graceful curving horn, off which the gale blew puffs of snow-dust like smoke. What a change from the manifold shades of colour, and more, from the concert of descending streams, that make this clough delightful in summer! The bottom was heaped up with drifts that made each step a muscular effort, and the careful pioneering of two alpenstocks did not save us from many a tumble into bog-holes filled with snow. Tired with the slow progression, two of us left the neighbourhood of the stream, and struggled up the fell-side towards the looming cliffs of Upper Tor. Since the snow was being continually blown down the hill, the higher we went the harder grew the surface, and therewithal the more slippery. Steps had to be kicked one by one with our hobnailed toes most of the way up, and a slip would have sent us on a long, swift slide. Not far up, a flock of grouse numbering several hundreds went off complaining, and we found many cup-shaped hollows in the snow, where these unfortunates had been spending the night. The last bit of climbing was up a couloir between two high buttresses of grit, and then we were on the top.

Where were the other pair, who had chosen to cut their way right up to the ice-bound gorge of the Grindsbrook? They were lost to sight in the misty gulf beneath us, across which we looked to the long snow-slope of Grindsbrook Knoll. The vast sheet of white was not unrelieved by zones and patches of shading, the buried heather marked the snow with a delicate etching, and every undulation changed the character of the surface. Areas of unsullied white bordered on areas of grey, and the frozen snow had been diapered by the graver of the sleet-laden wind into multitudinous patterns. Over every watercourse the upper snow curved like a wave; and on every hill-brow the "cornice," several feet wide, and whole furlongs in length, was a startling proof of the cohesiveness and plasticity of this product of the clouds. In one place we trespassed on the cornice, and nearly went through into the deep ravine at the head of the clough. The walking was a good deal better than it would have been in summer, the bog being covered with a hard pavement, very different from the soft snow near the dale. Instead of the "groughs" full of inky water and mud, we had arches of snow and wind-fretted canopies, under which there was shelter from the intolerable blast.

Now we caught sight of our comrades nearing the edge. One was cutting steps up the frozen slope with an ice-axe, and evidently selecting the most "sporting" route. A burst of sunshine shot through just then, and illumined the whole length of the deep, winding clough, touching the ridge beyond Edale with soft gold, and suffusing with roseate hues the pale wisps and wreaths of mist that floated in the gulf beneath us. We made a gallant attempt to get the camera into action, but the flying clouds shut out the picture before our numbed fingers had fixed it up. Then, after lunching comfortlessly under the lea of a big rock, we set off nor'-nor'-west, the leader marching at the head of the file, compass in hand. Once only the mist lifted a moment, and Hey Ridge with its tors beyond the Ashop glimmered and vanished.

By some mistake we came out on the edge of Crowden Clough, a long and dreary way from the Downfall, and some one uttered the fatal suggestion that we might go down here. As yet we had made but a half-hearted attempt to cross the Scout to Kinder Downfall; yet no one felt the spirit of protest, all had had enough. We stood on the edge of just such another steep slope, covered with hard snow, as the one we had ascended with so much toil and trouble. A glissade was proposed. Three of us had only read about that thrilling Alpine game, and we trembled; glissading, we understood, played terrible havoc with beginners. When, however, our captain shot off gracefully down the giddy incline, steering a course easily and confidently with the handle of his ice-axe, a second followed timidly, and now all four had taken the plunge. Sitting with legs firmly advanced, the surface snow collecting under us in a kind of natural sled, we were off like toboggans, with so little sense of friction we might have been shooting through air. But our steering was inadequate; to handle a long alpenstock as rudder needs practice. We rocketed off sideways, on our backs and on our faces, finishing with a wild plunge into the drifts at the bottom. Who shall describe the exhilarating thrill of that first mad rush? We were almost tempted to re-ascend and begin again. And after our long trudge back through miles of drifts, after dinner at the Nag's Head, one enthusiast, drunk with the charms of glissading, borrowed a tea-tray, and beguiled the twilight hour with startling evolutions on the snow, not more to his own delectation than to the joy and wonder of the villagers.

It was winter yet in the upper regions, though in the dales it was a hot day in spring, when I got my first glimpse of the Downfall and the glories of Kinder's western edges. On this occasion, it may as well be confessed, I had not armed myself with a licence to view these carefully treasured landscapes; but trusting partly to sound legs and lungs, and partly to the known frailties of keepers, I had deliberately committed the sin of trespassing. Howbeit, in those days, before the famous controversy as to the right of way over Mill Hill, the crime was not a heinous one, if you consider how wide a stretch of superb country was nominally forbidden to the public. Having gotten a long way up the Kinder stream from Hayfield without let or hindrance, I was suddenly aware of two figures striding rapidly along the hillside at the distance of several fields above me. Obviously they were bent on meeting me at a point farther up the brook. At the next wall, therefore, the highest on this side, I took the precaution to change my direction, and creeping uphill to the left under its cover, I found myself, after a tough pull, on the open moor, with nothing near me but a few sheep and many scores of startled grouse, that whirred almost from beneath my feet, with a noise that I thought would attract the enemy. But so far as they were concerned I had slippd away into the mist, and I saw them no more.

This unpremeditated digression took me to the north end of the Scout, where a long, dark edge stretches east, crowned at intervals with oddly-shaped stacks and towers of swarthy grit. My way was south, along the western edge, to the Downfall, a mile away. As I skirted the crags, ness after ness jutted out from the long, mountainous escarpment into the golden haze that shut out the world; and, in the deep bays and coves between, late fields of snow gleamed in the shadow and glistened in the sun. The russet hues and ruddy gold of the grass patches covered the fell-side with warm colour, and where Nab Brow loomed dimly through the haze, seemed to stain the very air and the sunshine. Never did the Witch's Pool look more visionary—a patch of flashing blue, ethereal as a patch of sky. Then the black gorge of the Downfall opened beneath me, but the fall itself was shrunk to a jet of pellucid water flinging prismatic tints on the crags that enfold it.

The dread of keepers was still in my soul, and without halting to eat the coveted sandwich I pushed on up the main stream, now merely a chain of pools issuing from a tunnel beneath thick beds of snow. The top of these, for the snow was hard and firm, offered the most convenient path, far better than the humpy moss-hags to right and left; and I went south-east and north-east, up one stream and down another, till I was safely across the bog. Then in a nook of Fairbrook Clough, the combe that descends through fold after heathery fold of the great hillside to the Ashop, with a rillet of snow-fed water spurting deliciously from a fall hard by, I ate my belated lunch.

A winter ascent of Kinder Scout has now become an annual institution. But we have not always found the great fall buried in ice and snow. The Scout is perhaps at its worst during a mild winter, as on one December day when we saw it in a storm. There had been no fall of snow, but heavy rains had swollen the Kinder stream to a roaring torrent. In the upper regions, outlines of cliff and watercourse faded imperceptibly into the mist, all accurate measures of size and altitude were abolished, so that as the water came down out of the unseen and foamed over the rocks before being engulfed in the gloom below, we could almost imagine ourselves gazing on the fume and turmoil of a Norwegian fos. The Downfall was magnificent, for a hurricane was blowing sheer against the spot where, nearly 2,000ft. above sea-level, it plunges over the crags. The instant the stream touched the brink it was caught by the gale, with the effect, often seen in the mountains, that the water was hurled upwards bodily in a white

Photo by   *G.A. Fowkes, Derby.*

THE TOP OF KINDER SCOUT IN WINTER.

Photo by

SUMMER IN THE CLOUGHS OF KINDER SCOUT.

Richard Keene, Ltd., Derby.

column, whilst in the lulls of the blast it dashed hither and thither, as if directed from place to place by some mighty hand, drenching the rocks with spray. The tortured stream raged and leapt like a furious animal. It seemed a living thing.

Two of us found an easy passage up the cliff, but the others got into difficulties, and did not reach the top for some time. We two might have been standing on a rock-bound coast, staring into the surf and rack of a storm. The uproar drowned our voices. Eyes could not pierce the weltering mist, the roar of many waters came up from below, the wind bellowed in the rents and hollows of the cliff, and every streamlet as it tumbled over the edge was blown aloft like the spray from a blow-hole, and driven furiously over the face of the moor. When the missing scramblers appeared, we set off across the bog, up the river-bed for nearly a mile, and then, by the compass, over the watershed to the Fairbrook. To steer a way across this wilderness of quaking bogs, deep and slippery water-channels, and thick-set humps of peaty earth, is one of the severest tests of a man's ability to use the compass. He is bound to consult the needle at every few yards, for to take many steps together in anything like a straight line is impossible; one simply blunders on among the gullies and ridges, and corrects one's aberrations from time to time. On a clear day it is bad enough; but when we are immersed in a current of thick, soaking mist, and the fluid bog is more fluid than ever, all our faculties must be on the alert to save us from utter bewilderment.

The anniversary of that day has been celebrated by a long series of rambles over the Scout. Sometimes we have found the Downfall entirely frozen up, a sheet of crystal flung in translucent folds across the rugged

B

wall.   But once again we encountered weather as uncomfortable as that just described.   Among the dozen in our party were several who perhaps had never been on a peat-moss in their lives, and certainly never in any but the finest summer weather.   They had heard great tales about Kinder Scout in winter, and were ambitious to see the highest spot in their county under the grandest conditions.   At Hayfield it was not exactly fine, yet not rainy; by the time we had passed the Downfall we were nearly as wet as if we had climbed straight through it.

> " They found it too rough in the bed of the clough,
>   And too steep on the rocky hill-side,
>   And they thought that the cliffs were a little too tough,
>   And the moss-hags a great deal too wide." *

Up the bed of the Kinder river, over the morass, and down the " rind " or waterway of the Crowden Brook, was for the neophytes a weary and heart-breaking struggle.   When we pointed out the slimy pools and sloughs that represent the watershed of England, they were so disgusted with the foulness of earth and heaven that they protested it looked more like a cowshed.   At the point where the stream cuts through the edge, it plunges under a bridge or tunnel of mounded boulders; we went through this natural culvert too, and on down the precipitous ravine, jumping with the water from ledge to ledge.   The inn that day seemed to have every room filled with people in the various stages of saturation and evaporation; it was like a Turkish bath.   You could not get near a fire for drenched clothes.   A number had gone to bed; through a door we saw two men with a jacket apiece sitting up in bed, and playing " nap " on an inverted footbath.   And when our own party, clothed chiefly

---

* Kyndwr Club Ballad.

in garments hurriedly purchased at the village hosiery, sat down to dinner, the steam of roast beef and the steam of drying raiment were blissfully commingled. The neophytes never paid another visit to Kinder; they thought one such experience in one ordinary lifetime enough for reasonable men.

But Kinder Scout is not everlastingly muffled in clouds, and beaten upon by rains and winds, even in winter. And winter in the Peak has one especial beauty. In summer many of the streams are extinct, their channels are ugly scars, and a walk through the dusty heather provokes a thirst that cannot be quenched without descending to the dales. This characteristic is more familiar, perhaps, in the limestone regions. The Lathkill, for instance, in summer is not a river, but a chain of pools and streamlets, with long reaches so dry that a lawn grows on the bed of a mill-pool. But look at it in winter. Walk across the gray and arid uplands of the limestone till you come suddenly on the brink of Lathkill Dale, and far down in the profound rift you see the water running over the trailing grasses and weeds. It is like a living emerald, a serpentine ribbon of green light, waving and flashing between the crags and the leafless woods. And down every clough on Kinder pours a limpid brook, slightly stained with peat, full of deep pools, full of plunging cascades, and meeting at every wrinkle in the hillside a silver rillet flowing through the lustrous green of bog grass and mountain mosses.

In order to complete the circuit of Kinder Scout, I will now run over the ground covered in a ramble from Edale to the Snake by a party of five, one day when winter had gone, but summer had hardly appeared yet on the bleak moorlands. Two of the five had recently been caught in an innocent act of trespass by a redoubtable farmer, who had been dissuaded only by bribery from walking them off to Bakewell police-court. With their nerves unsteadied by this experience, they listened with quaking hearts to our talk about fierce and implacable gamekeepers; and when it was pointed out as a queer coincidence that the brow we were ascending is called "The Nab," the omen struck them as full of terrible significance. Little was said about a certain document that one of us carried, which was supposed to be a powerful talisman for softening the obdurate hearts of keepers. We climbed the Nab at a brisker pace than we should have managed without this spur, and were soon too far up the slope to tempt pursuit, had there been any fear of it. Then we climbed the craggy side of Ringing Rocher, whose tapering gable presents the appearance of a fine cone towards Grindsbrook Clough.

We were skirting the rocky rim of that great hollow. From its far depths, the song of the Grindsbrook came rippling up as through a vast, resonant chamber, whose echoes multiplied the notes to infinity. But for the long red rubbish heaps that fall from the two black ravines at the head of the clough, the hollow was full of shadow, and its features were confounded together by the dark haze. A beautiful green dell, covered with a deep forest of waving bracken, dipped between us and the black cliffs of Nether Tor. We were surprised to notice the traces of an old cart-track crossing it, at the end of which, right under the edge, was a deserted quarry, some 1,700ft. above sea-level, one of the most inaccessible I have ever seen.

We had not come out on scrambling intent, but a fine buttress enticed us to avoid the more humdrum ways of getting to the plateau. It looked very simple, a short, tough struggle over a number of projecting

Photo by   G.A. Fowkes, Derby.

NETHER TOR – KINDER SCOUT.

shelves, and an easy scramble over rocks and heather to the top. So we innocently sent the youngest member of the party to try what we thought a suitable problem for beginners, and turned our attention to photography. How he got up without breaking his neck we never knew. At all events, when the two practised climbers came to the apparently easy part, we found ourselves in a fix, though one of us laid the blame on his nail-less boots, and the other on his hand, disabled by an accident on the Lake mountains. We used each other's shoulders and heads to stand on, in getting up two smooth, straight corners; and when we came to the rickety stones at the top, where the edge sloped out and was bare of holds, one let down a leg for the other to grip. We congratulated that young man on his courage and reproved his audacity.

We were now crossing the south-eastern promontory of the Scout, keeping inland so as to avoid the upper reaches of Jagger's Clough, skirting the slopes of Black Dean Edge, and crossing Black Dean Rind, which was waterless, the black surface of the peat-bogs being dry enough to walk upon. Then turning north-eastwards again, rising over the crests of bilberry hillocks and plunging into the troughs between, we made our way across the moss, and suddenly we were on the edge—Seal Edge. The whole Ashop valley was beneath us, and beyond it the eye roamed to the most distant confines of that wild desert which lies so romantically in the very middle of crowded England. A blue-grey haze mingled its heights and hollows, subduing the heather-clad fells, the deep shadowy cloughs, and the glaring patches of scree and naked rock, to one soft tint. Ridge beyond ridge lengthened out, like film beyond film of cloud, and between the ridges, in the inscrutable line of shadow, we knew that a river was foaming deep down in a rocky dale—the Alport, the Westend, and the Derwent. Only one distinct shape was there, the road in the Ashop valley, solitary and glaring white, a hint of human neighbourhood that made the solitudes beyond more profound and strange. High and far at the back of the region hung the dim mass of Bleaklow, with its vague miles of flat horizon, only a shade more solid than the clouds.

It was painfully dry on top. Not a brook had a pool of clean water left; even in the main channel of the Fairbrook the sand was perfectly dry, only a puddle or two of sour, green water lurking in cool nooks beneath the boulders. When we ate our lunch, we had to go without a drink; but the cool, refreshing breeze kept our thirst from becoming a torment, as it would have done had the day been hot. On the frowning ramparts of Seal Edge, we picked out tempting corners here and there for a pull up with the arms, and smooth clefts for back-and-knee work, our foe, the unruly wind, striving hard to fling us off our balance at exposed points. One man got into a curious quandary in trying to reach the summit of as whimsical a clump of gnarled and weather-beaten rocks as even the grit can produce. Unable to put his head out of shelter, for fear of being blown off his hand-hold, he tried to come down, and thought a certain long, slanting shelf was the easiest way. But a big rock overhung the shelf closely, pushing half his body over the edge, where it hung unsupported. First he tried to do it on his back, then he returned and made another attempt, wriggling face downwards. One arm and one leg pawed at random over the smooth rock beneath, vainly feeling for a ledge; there was no vestige of such a thing for 12ft. down. So the rest of the party, enjoying the absurdity of his situation, came to the rescue. One climbed up to the leg, and another to the pendent arm, while the rest got a piece of him from the safe end of the shelf, and so he was gently lowered, all helpless and upside-down, on to the heather.

We crossed the deep clough of the Fairbrook, and climbed the fell-side to Fairbrook Naze, the sharp and precipitous headland, grandest of all the crags on Kinder, that dominates the vale of the Ashop, and marks the termination of the eastern and northern edges. We would gladly have explored its straight, swart masses of unfractured rock, the ugly rifts that cut into it from foot to crest, and the cliffs beyond, all convulsed and shivered to their bases, bristling with splintered projections. But our time was too short, and it was not till later that we had an opportunity to try the mettle of what seemed then to be the finest set of scrambles on Kinder Scout. From the Naze the long north edge runs westwards above the sources of the Ashop, toward Mill Hill, where the path made by the Rights of Way Society comes within a furlong or two of the Scout. Towers and pinnacles and grotesque simulacra of artificial things, all weathered out of the dark grit, mark the crest of the slopes as far as the eye can see. We ran down through the beginnings of a smart shower to the rough cutting in which the Ashop flows, crossing which we were once more on a beaten track, and soon came in sight of the hospitable Snake, the natural goal of most wanderers on Kinder Scout.

II.

IN THE HEART OF THE PENNINE.

THERE are three localities in Derbyshire distinguished by the name of Alport, but to judge by the guide-books Alport River and Alport Clough are the least known, though they represent some of the most typical and most impressive scenery in the Peak. Travellers on the road to the Kinder Scout hospice, the Snake Inn, are liable to overlook the narrow cleft in the hills down which the Alport flows from its wild moorland fastness to join the Ashop. Here a few cottages cling together among some straggling trees, with the bleak, storm-swept moors stretching up and up on every side. A rough road leads a little way along the tributary dale to the highest farmstead, and is worth following so far in order to get one glimpse of the stern defile that the little river has hewn through these lofty moorlands. But if you would go further you must be a well-seasoned bog-trotter, for beyond this point you leave rights of way and everything pertaining to humanity far behind, and you will hardly see a house or a stone wall till you are in sight of Yorkshire.

We were spending a week-end at the Snake, when a chance meeting gave us permission to visit this sacred territory of the grouse. Four had crossed the Scout on the previous day, and two had gone home, unfortunately leaving us, by inadvertence, without a compass. In the evening we two strolled up the Glossop road, up

Lady Clough, and on to the summit level, where the road crosses the high ground culminating in distant Bleaklow Head. It was a calm, roseate evening, but it could not soften the harsh and misanthropic features of the far-stretching peat-moss, across which the road wends its way, with only a shallow ditch to separate it from the tussocks of peat and heather and the quaking sloughs. This is the place to anatomise melancholy in. Keats and the author of " Il Penseroso " give us sweet and voluptuous landscapes. Would not their melancholy have had a deeper tinge, or would it have been silenced utterly, had they meditated their theme in this dreary waste? Yet there is a powerful charm for some of us, in some of our moods at all events, in such a spot as this. Is it the stillness, with the faint suggestion of music in the quiet rillets, or the strange harmonies of blue sky and the infinitely graduated browns of the moorland, or is it merely the intense solitude? We feel the charm, but what it is we know not; it is incommunicable. As Thomas Hardy says so finely of Egdon Heath, night seemed to be an emanation from the earth. The moor was dark, while the air and sky were still alive with light, as we returned downhill towards the cheerily shining windows of the inn.

Next morning we were not in a hurry to start, for the weather was most unpropitious. When at length we walked down to the confluence of Ashop and Alport we were in two minds whether to venture into the wilderness or trudge comfortably down to Bamford Station. Rain threatened, a mist wrapped the hill-tops, and we had no compass. This was a serious difficulty in the circumstances, though we were not without maps. However, the next fifteen minutes saw us fairly launched, the last inhabited house was put behind us, and we plodded over the last bit of meadow land, earnestly considering the warnings of an old keeper who lived at the upper farmstead. The Alport looks the perfection of a trout stream, exquisitely clear, and full of alternating runs and pools; but not the shadow of a fin could we see. High on our right we saw indistinctly the fantastic projections and fragments of an old landslip that are nicknamed "Castles," but the mists soon roofed the valley over completely, and we beheld little more than the river with its rocky channel, and the steep sides of the now contracted clough rising almost like walls on either hand. For many miles Alport Clough is a V-shaped trench, hundreds of feet deep, cut through the elevated moorlands, and the slopes are so severe and the shaly soil is so slippery that we found the river bed to be the safest footpath. Though full, the river left a fair margin of water-worn rock, and the going was not bad for the most part. Above the meadows near its mouth the Alport is a Southron burn—swift, lacking in pools, and containing more respectable waterfalls than any other stream in the county. One of the prettiest is a miniature Fall of Tummel, a series of rapids, comprising one good jump and some fine twisting eddies in the corners. We got wet in fording just here, the crag on our bank driving us across. Then a more regular fall made a barrier right across the bottom of the clough. I was struggling hard to clamber up the rocks, heavily draped with moss and weed, whilst a jet from the waterfall shot down my sleeve, when my comrade suddenly appeared on the top, having circumvented the obstacle somehow, and gave me a helping hand.

Where tributaries come in, so narrow is the ravine, they break out in the wall high above the main stream and create small cascades. One of these, into which we peered by scrambling up the opposite wall, had the look of a huge funnel or drain cut artificially into a bigger one. It was like peeping into the geological workshop and seeing Nature's methods and contrivances without the disguising influence of weathering and vegetation. The deep and winding defile is several miles in length, and only one valley of any size joins it—a valley that has much the same character impressed on it by the shaly rock. We found the hours of wading and scrambling so amply satisfying that we swore, whatever befell, not to go back that way. Yet when we saw the clough rising to the level of the surrounding moors, the difficulty we had anticipated of finding our way at once became serious. We had risen out of the region of wet mist into a mist that was dry but very dense, and we had left the guiding walls of the clough behind us. Just at the critical point the Ordnance map divides, and we were quite unable to trace out the likeliest of the head-streams that here unite to form the Alport. Lacking a compass and without a sun to direct us, we had to make shift with the wind for a guide. It was at best a doubtful one, but we made up our minds as to the quarter it was blowing from when we entered the valley three hours ago, and, assuming for the nonce that it had not shifted, we resolved to keep it blowing in our left ears until we got over the Bleaklow moors to the other side. Bleaklow Head, the second highest summit in Derbyshire, lay somewhere ahead of us, but all the view we got was a few perches of boggy soil and the grey encompassing mist whirling by in masses of varying density. The ground as we rose grew more and more like the boggy plain on top of Kinder. Countless hillocks of peat sticking up in every direction made one think of a field ploughed and cross-ploughed into gigantic furrows, with broken ridges from five to ten

feet high rising into tottering heaps a few yards apart.
This kind of ground is as bad as a thick wood for
finding your way, even in clear weather. Abundant
snow-wreaths lay in the hollows; and, in order to avoid
the besetting danger of making a circuit and returning
blindly in the direction we had come by, we cut arrows
on these patches to show our course.

Wandering among the sluggish rivulets, apparently
bound for nowhere in particular, that form a bewildering
network at the source of the streams, we found Bleaklow
Head at last. Our prospect was still limited to a few
yards, yet we had the satisfaction of verifying our
position. We consumed a few morsels of lunch as a
tribute to the occasion, but it was too cold for loitering,
and in a few minutes we were pressing on over the
watershed. Watershed is a geographical term that
would be very hard to define physically on this broad
table-land. We had gone astray down many promising
ravines and doubled back on our general direction many
times before we got into a watercourse that led decisively
downhill. Lonely and unspeakably solemn as are these
broad spaces of treeless earth and smokeless sky on a
bright summer's day, they overwhelm the mind with
a more powerful sense of solitude and helplessness, when
mist imprisons the eye and leaves the imagination
unfettered. Once a doleful whistle shrilled a few yards
away, startling us with its apparently human note,
though we knew in a moment it must be a curlew's
cry. Save this, naught broke the silence but the
ceaseless rush of the gale over the heather bushes, a
sound that is like the pauseless sweep of a swift, smooth
flood of water.

Crowden Station, on the Great Central, was our
objective point, but several miles of the roughest ground
intervened; and with our erratic guide, old Boreas, who

still blew furiously, there were endless chances of
wandering a league or two astray. The next sound
that broke the diapason of wind and herbage was a
train whistle. Where was it? Glossop, Penistone, or
some outlandish place far from any station? Presently
the ground fell more rapidly, the mist grew perceptibly
thinner. Suddenly we became aware of a deep and
rugged ravine close on our left, with a straight slope
on the far side that in the obscurity looked terribly high
and precipitous. Later on we ascertained that this was
Wildboar Clough. Then a startling vision rushed upon
us out of the mist. Right in front, dim at first and
wan as a mirage, a great sheet of water extended its
surface, seemingly as ample as a highland loch, with
bare hills towering darkly on its distant shore. A
little thought told us that this could be nothing else
than one of the biggest of the Woodhead reservoirs,
magnified by the conditions of the atmosphere to far
beyond its actual size. It is in reality nearly two miles
in length, and the wind coming up the dale was
driving a white line of surf towards the upper end.
Soon all our doubts as to our whereabouts were put to
rest, and we congratulated ourselves on having come
over this difficult and unknown country, in a fog, to
the very haven we had steered for.

III.

WINTER AND SPRING ON THE YORKSHIRE AND DERBYSHIRE EDGES.

WHAT gives so rare a charm to a walk along the Derbyshire and Yorkshire edges, is the sustained contrast between the gloom and austerity of the moors, on the one hand, and the contiguous beauty of woods and spinneys or of pastoral valleys, on the other. Even the immeasurable contrasts of sea and shore are scarcely more vivid or more enchanting, and not many coastlines are grander than the grandest of our abrupt, shattered, and weatherworn escarpments of millstone grit, such, for instance, as Stanage Edge, Higgar Tor, and Froggatt Edge. That is how it strikes one in summer, but in winter the contrast between the arctic moorlands, where life is well-nigh extinct, and the comparatively genial dale, is not less apparent.

Bamford Edge, one morning in February, 1900, was a place where few people would be mad enough to spend an hour unless urged by dire necessity. The air was thick with flying arrows of sleet and updriven snow, no fog could be more blinding. Through the white turmoil loomed, by instants, vague phantoms of cliff and boulder, then in an instant were wiped away again. Across the open, the wind swept in a steady, irresistible current that staggered us, as with bowed heads we struggled onwards. Then, nearer the edge, it was broken into furious gusts and eddies, that whirled about one with insidious violence, and made us keep at a safe distance from the brink. The moment our party of five had debouched from the wood of pine and larch that shelters the lane up the hill from Bamford, conversation ceased by one consent, and each man's attention was concentrated on himself. For to maintain a footing even, amongst the ruts and holes completely hidden by the snow, with the hurricane lashing and twisting one, was work enough for a man. Each felt a sneaking desire to skulk behind his neighbour, for the blast seemed to go through our clothes as if they were muslin, and to whistle between our ribs. Blizzards, they say, do not occur on this side of the Atlantic; but without quibbling about words we might, surely, offer our friends from New York, even here in the very middle of England, a very satisfactory substitute for the home product.

After stumbling—for the snow made it useless to speculate whether the next step would alight on a rock or in a bog-hole—and struggling to our feet with difficulty, we reached at length the summit of the Edge. Our design had been to go across the Derwent moors towards Bradfield, a district new to some of the party; but the weather and fresh air, that were all we could expect to enjoy to-day, could be had here without going farther afield, so we halted under the lea of a snow-wreathed crag and tried to eat a sandwich, whilst we took counsel together. Even here, sitting in a deep drift, and surrounded by a wall of snow, we were not safe from the enemy, who pelted us from every chink and crevice, flying up our sleeves and filling our gloves, if we were rash enough to take them off. One man sustained a curious frost-bite, the skin coming off one of his hands the week after.

The discussion was curt and decisive. Only one man out of five said a word in favour of going on, and his boldness was only the obstinate temper of minorities. Again we faced the volleys of frozen darts. We rounded the crags and made our way to a depression in the edge; for only here and there was a descent practicable. A few yards below the crest the force of the gale was palpably less. We leaned backwards, digging our heels into deep snow, for we were now plunging into the drifts that had been raked and swept from the plateau and flung in heaps down the hillside. Our progress was something between a run and a series of jumps and stumbles. Most of us came to grief. Among the rest, the photographer took an unpremeditated header into the soft snow, his camera shooting over his shoulders; but neither instrument nor owner was damaged by the fall. Soon we found ourselves within the shelter of a larch wood, where the gale was barely felt. But though we had withdrawn from the battle, we could see what rude warfare was raging a few hundred feet above our heads, for the snow was continually lifted in sheets from the hill crest, and hurled aloft in clouds to join the one great cloud that enveloped the upper regions. And we ourselves bore from foot to pate obvious traces of the recent conflict. The frozen sleet had stung our faces as if it would fetch the blood, gradually encasing our cheeks with a rigid vizor of ice that made smiling difficult. We took refuge at Yorkshire Bridge Inn, at the bottom of the hill, where each was admitted only after the courteous landlord had raked him fore and aft with a brushwood besom and chopped the icicles off his whiskers with a big pocket-knife, a painful purification that had to be finished in front of a roaring fire. The photographer, emboldened by the descent to a milder elevation, and by the proximity of a bar-room fire and other stimulants, shot off all his plates, just outside the front door; and then, having got rid of his camera, cheerfully acquiesced in a proposal to ascend Derwent Edge.

So far we had had winter at its rudest and most intolerable; now we were to see winter in all its ethereal beauty. By noon the storm had moderated, although the wind was as boisterous as ever on the hills. The clouds had been swept away, the sun shone from a sky of clearest azure, and over the world of luminous white was shed a flood of sunlight more brilliant than that of midsummer. We set out for the Ladybower, along the main road in the valley; our feet were the first to mar its virgin smoothness. On this side, Win Hill always looks majestic. With his abrupt eastern slopes covered with snow he seemed a real mountain. But what fascinated us more than anything else to-day, was the long streamer of snow trailing far across the sky from his summit. All day the snow was driven up between the topmost rocks, and across the heavens sunwards, like a volcano's plume of smoke or the cloud banner from a seaward peak. In all the vast heaving landscape of frozen hills, this was the wonderful sight that kept the eyes spellbound.

From Cut-throat Bridge we plodded through the drifts towards Derwent Edge, and soon encountered the fury of the wind again. In the forenoon, when charged with frozen sleet, it had been too much for human flesh to stand; but with the sky clear and the sun shining, the gale was full of exhilaration. Nor were we much put out when the drifts ensnared our feet. One man who plunged inadvertently into a ditch filled with snow was the means of discovering a new and delightful pastime. Five minutes later the whole party might have been seen madly taking headers or pulling somebody out by the legs. And when at last anxiety about train time turned us downhill again, strange modes of locomotion

c

were adopted over the huge drifts; one man was observed swimming head foremost down a slope where the snow lay breast deep.

Never even in the mountains had we beheld such marvellous effects of snow and sunlight. A casual gust would send up a pillar of eddying white that caught the light splendidly before falling far over the fields. The hills and the horizons were marked out in lines of living light, ribbons of light that whirled in perpetual motion, the which were really whirling ribbons of snow lifted by the wind and shot through and through with sunbeams. And then there were places where the sky's intense blue waned into grey and white, and the pure slopes of snow melted away ever so gently into a pure opaline haze, so that no eye could tell the boundary of earth and heaven. But who shall describe the indescribable? That day was one of the ineffable days of creation, such as we only experience once now and again throughout the years, though its memory will often lure us away to the snowy moorlands on days when sober people are snuggling round the fire.

Such are the contrasts of winter. It so happened that our next visit to Bamford Edge was in spring-time. Except that there was no snow and no excruciating cold, the aspect of things as we walked out from the woods on to the moor was strikingly similar. A gale was blowing; and as it came in contact with the high ground to windward it spread a great cloud to leeward over the hills. We made our way to the edge and looked over. There was little more to see than when last we were up here, only the looming crags, and the ragged slopes of heather and scattered rocks, dying away indefinably into misty space. We ate our lunch and smoked a pipe underneath a ledge of grit, and debated whether we should wait for a change in the weather. We made up our minds to get away from this hopeless spot, at all events; and with compass as guide we steered into the eye of the wind eastwards for Stanage Edge. The moor slopes gently downwards, almost imperceptibly, toward that lofty escarpment. No drearier piece of landscape could be imagined, unless it be drearier still when there is no mist to cover its ugliness. Right in the middle of the bare, featureless waste there stretched, between us and the cliffs of Stanage, a broad morass, whose vivid greens and yellows, peaty pools and foaming rivulets, were a relief to the wearied eye. For a while the mist grew more rare, and through it we could discern the savage slopes of bog and bilberry, rock-bestrewn, that lead up to Stanage Edge, though the Edge itself was yet in the clouds. The peat-moss was alive with birds; plovers and curlews, whinchats and larks flew up as we approached; the grouse rose suddenly from under our noses, the cuckoo called vociferously across the moor; and many a hare, neither white nor brown, but just changing his suit, went bounding up the hill, and stopped impudently to stare at us from a safe distance.

Before long the compass was dispensed with, for we could see the unfenced road from Bamford to Redmires, and beyond it one block of gritstone as big as a house, and two or three others hardly smaller, one of which, the map averred, was the Buckstone. Then we came across a highly picturesque flock of sheep at graze on the moorland, and the two photographers spent half an hour stalking these suspicious animals, up hill and down dale, in vain efforts to get a snapshot; whilst the brace of scramblers passed the time in a rock climb on the finely shaped crags that overhang the road. We are here on the dividing line between the desert and the vale. From our feet, in one direction, stretched

the sombre heath, far, far away, farther than the eye
could distinguish things in the dim haze, crested with
lines of crag, furrowed with groughs and moss-hags,
and culminating in grand misty shapes like mountain
peaks, so magnified were the moorland heights by the
atmosphere, in the direction of Bamford and Derwent
Edges. The cone of Win Hill rose end on in the hazy
distance, stately and magnificent, and the vague edges
of Kinder looked immensely higher than they really
were.   In the other direction, we looked down a sudden
cleft in the hillside, a clough full of trees and copses,
through which the brook descends from the morass
we had just crossed into the wooded valley above
Hathersage.   Very tempting were these glimpses of
rich woodlands and hanging pastures, but our desires
travelled on to where edge after edge and headland after
headland advanced their clear outlines out of the cloudy
waste, and towered superbly over the vale of Derwent.

   We kept to the high road until we reached the noblest
part of Stanage Edge, a long half-mile of black, massy
cliff, overhanging a wood-sprinkled hillside.   Rifted
and shaken by ancient frosts, with mighty blocks flung
down the slopes, and mighty scars remaining to show
whence they were torn, this grand old bulwark still
rises straight and solid, as if it would endure the storms
and frosts of untold centuries to come.   It is built of
the hardest grit, that weathers slowly, presenting sharp
edges instead of rounded, crumbly bosses; its huge
rectangular masses look like a wall built by Titans
From the foot of this grim black cliff the slopes of red
dead bracken and green young bracken fall away to
meet a crowd of beeches that climb the hill in straggling
clusters.   The beech leaves at this time of the year are
delicate and diaphanous and of a luminous green, too
delicate a green to last many weeks.   The ruddy brown

A Scramble on Black Edge, part of Stanage Edge.

Photo by

W. Meakin, Newthorpe, Notts.

The BURBAGE BROOK IN ITS MOORLAND COURSE.

of the bracken, the exquisite freshness of the wildwood, and the depths of sombre green in the woods of pine below, give us again that absorbing idea of contrast with the sternness and blackness of the Edge.

At the end of the crags is a long-deserted quarry. Scores of millstones lie about the hillside, as if giants had been playing at quoits, and a ruinous cottage contains the dismantled forge where, no doubt, the tools were repaired and sharpened for the quarrymen when this was still a lucrative industry. And now, a mile away in front, Higgar Tor rises out of a hollow that breaks the continuity of the edges. Its individuality of form is striking. We thought at first we had come to Carl's Wark, so like a rock-fortress is this solitary, cliff-girt tableland, but we had to cross the tor and look down from its farther edges before we saw the old stronghold, rising abruptly in the midst of the wild upland valley beyond. This forlorn refuge of the pre-historic Peak men crowns the top of a steep little hill, and is protected along three sides by natural cliffs, while the fourth is guarded by a rampart of large boulders, carefully laid in courses, and, though unshaped and uncemented, as firm as the natural rock. It is a mournful, inhospitable place, and the people who fled hither must surely have been hard pressed to leave the fertile dales for this bare spot. However, the fort looks strong enough to hold out as long as provender lasted, against the weapons of the stone age. Under the cliff wall the Burbage Brook runs across the wild hollow, admirable type of a Peakland stream, with its peaty-brown waters and bounding strength of current, and in the suddenness of the descent from its savage home to the beauty and fertility below the edges. The change comes all at once where the Sheffield and Manchester road crosses the brook. There, at the bridge, it leaps

over Millstone Edge; it has left the stony, heathery
moor, the haunt of grouse and mountain hare, where no
villages of man have been since yonder crag-built
fortress became a ruin; and all at once the stream finds
itself in another climate, in the midst of flowers and
ferns, and of a forest as rich as Sherwood. What other
little stream sees so great a transformation in so brief
a course, or has been the silent witness of so much
historical romance? For though the tragedies that were
enacted in remote ages, where the rock-fortress towers
over the stream, have been forgotten, tragic memories
still cling to the ruins of Padley Hall, below in the
dale.

Before entering Padley Woods, we turn aside towards
the fine old Tudor hostelry of Fox House Inn. Going
in at the side door from the court-yard, we step back,
as it were, three centuries, into the England of Queen
Bess. When we came out, the fair weather had gone
for the day. The further hills were fast disappearing,
and the moors re-asserting their wonted sullenness.
Against the dark welter of the rain clouds, Higgar Tor
and Carl's Wark towered up the one behind the other,
the hill-fort proud and threatening, with ramparts still
unbreached by its only foes for so many centuries, the
storms and frosts; and the mightier hill overtopping it
by head and shoulders, its flat top also encinctured by
Nature's fortification, and room enough thereon to
encamp an army. Their craggy forms seemed to rise
higher and dilate as the blackness swept over them;
anon they grew fainter and fainter until they were
entirely blotted out.

IV.

OVER BLEAKLOW HEAD TO THE SOURCES OF THE DERWENT.

ALL yesterday afternoon we had been disporting ourselves, and rubbing holes in our clothes on the needles, chockstones and face-climbs of a gritstone edge in Yorkshire. Strenuous exercise had been succeeded by a long and late evening of song—the songs that climbers sing—and then, when the matutinal birds were piping between five and six, we had been torn reluctantly from our beds to catch an unseasonable train. But two miles through the bracken and bluebells of a dewy wood were as refreshing as a cold bath, and the clear morning air soon washed the sleep from our eyes. One sad incident occurred at the station that was to cast a gloom over the luncheon hour presently. A member of the party left a fat package of sandwiches behind in the booking-office, the rations of two men and a half, only finding out the mishap when the train had started.

Two others, unnerved by the extent of our programme and by the inhospitable look of the Ordnance Survey map, got out at Dunford Bridge, preferring a locality where roads are not unknown, nor houses of refreshment quite unheard-of institutions. Howbeit, their experiences were far from proving so tame as they anticipated; for whoso ventures on the moors that lie about Featherbed Moss must needs leave it to Fortune to decide just where and when he will return to the macadamised world. At present their intention was to meet us about noon, near the head of the Derwent valley.

The remnant, numbering five, went on to Crowden Station, and there lost no time in crossing railway and highway on to the shaggy slopes under Lawrence Edge and Rollick Stones. We are in the moorlands at once. Tracts of ragged copse-land, slopes covered with heather and young bracken, and slopes of coarse grass, all more or less boggy and strewn with rocks, sweep up in broken curves to the craggy edge, with scarcely a field of tilth or meadow to separate the highway from the wilderness. We climbed rapidly to the first edge; but it was hot work, and we were thankful for the lightness of our rücksacks.

Behind the edge, we found ourselves on a vast table-land, sloping upwards very gently, dimpled here and there by little dells, and trenched by streams that cut their way through the peaty ground towards the deeper trench of Wildboar Clough on our right. The dense, rank grass that lines the hollows looks as soft as down, and covers the ground with a deep, elastic cushion, soft to lie on, but a hindrance to the feet. In the middle of every dell is a patch of glossy green, that shivers from side to side if a step comes too near. Over such ground it was impossible to keep up a brisk pace; yet in an hour the valley of Longdendale, in which the Woodhead reservoirs expand their broad sheets of water, was out of sight, and we were catching only distant glimpses of the hills beyond, clouds hanging low over their broad backs and whelming the dales in shadow.

And now, as far as we can see, the melancholy moors surround us—dark, silent, and apparently illimitable. Though nearly 2,000ft. above the sea, their vast flattened curves rise into no definite summits or hill-crests; blank of all significant features, they offer few points of measurement to the eye; only here and there the dark line of a gully or the edge of some hidden clough relieves the stern monotony, and reminds us of the deep valleys into which they fall. We sat in one of those soft grassy nooks, and ate our lunch, economising our allowance on account of the recent disaster to the sandwiches. Then we smoked, laughing and cracking jokes, profane intruders that we were into this sacred realm of " Silence and slow Time."

Hardly had we ended our meal and set on again when an ominous change came over the heavens. A violent storm threatened. The sky seemed to come down close over our heads, exhaling darkness; the dark heath itself was not more sombre. Only on one out-standing hill-top far away on the confines of Yorkshire and Lancashire a ray of sunlight fell, with a lurid effect; the gloom and the stillness were oppressive. Then a furious gust of wind came, and a rush of air from cold upper regions into the dull, close atmosphere beneath. Not a tree nor anything worth calling a bush existed for miles around, but we found a deep gully or " grough," and sought shelter underneath the eaves of heather overhanging its sides.

The storm never broke. No blue streamers of rain shot from the sullen sky, though thunderbolts and waterspouts threatened. We therefore concluded to go ahead. But it was fully an hour before the scowl in the heavens gave way to a milder expression, by which time we had trudged across weary miles of heather and forded innumerable brooklets, and ought now to be nearing Bleaklow Head. We proceeded carefully, trying from time to time with map and compass to determine our exact position. For miles that delightful sub-Alpine plant, the crowberry, grows in astonishing profusion, bringing to mind reminiscences of Skye and the eastern Grampians. Its graceful leafage covers the soil with a network of green, out of which the delicate white blooms shine starlike amid the prevalent browns of the moor. We were almost tempted to come again a month later to taste its delicious fruit.

Bleaklow Head has no imposing cairn or natural pile of lofty crag to mark its pre-eminence. It is simply one portion of a long bare hill extending east and west, with sides whose slopes are scarcely perceptible. It is the birthplace, however, of a great family of streams, several of which grow into important rivers, some running to the Irish Sea and some to the German Ocean. All over the watershed the water lies in deep trenches or groughs, often stagnant, often less water than slime. Taking precautions not to descend too precipitately, one gets to the oozy bottom and struggles up the steep yielding bank on the other side, clutches the cornice of bilberry on top, and climbs out on the moor, only to see a similar ditch gaping a few yards in front. With few exceptions, these channels run north and south with great regularity, right across our route, in some places opening into boggy tarns, to which we gave a wide berth.

By this time the menacing clouds had rolled up into mountains of cumulus, and from the clear blue sky the sun's rays beat on us fiercely, whilst under foot it was soft and wet. A very little of this and there was not a dry pair of legs in the party, for we often plunged in knee-deep, and boots and stockings were soaked and clogged with mire. Strange and various shifts were resorted to in desperate efforts to remedy this state of things. Two men adopted no half-measures, but doffed boots and stockings altogether, trudging recklessly on, through liquid and solid, barefoot. Two others merely slung their stockings across their shoulders to dry, and thrust bare feet into wet boots again. One man, who disdained the eccentricities of costume affected by tourists and mountaineers, and had come out attired in a decent suit of black, cheered us up wonderfully with the sight of his figure soberly plodding on through heather and morass, his socks flung over his shoulder, his trousers tucked up, displaying a lily-white ankle above his boots, a straw hat dangling from a piece of elastic, and a cap fixed over his grave spectacled face.

Gritstone weathers frequently into the same massy rectangular blocks as granite, which are wrought into those mimic piles of masonry that we are so familiar with on the tors and the edges, and the general configuration of the country has strong resemblances to granite districts. From Bleaklow Stones (2,062ft.) the view is that of a wilder, though less sombre and colourless, Dartmoor. The rock-crowned tors are there, assuming all fantastic likenesses; and the deep rents in the sky-line, where the Alport and Westend rivers cut a way through the elevated land, are singularly like Tavy Cleave and the grand defile of the Okement. In front of Bleaklow is a desolate hollow encircled by fells, the gathering-ground for these rivers, not unlike that trackless region of morass in the heart of Dartmoor, to reach whose centre, Cranmere Pool, is a feat on which the more adventurous tourist plumes himself greatly.

We were still a mile and a half from the end of our hill. Another eminence now appeared a long way in front, covered with a serried array of boulders, like some rude Stonehenge or a battered circle of prehistoric buildings. These were the Barrow Stones, we found by referring to the map, and the hill they surmounted was an important one geographically, for out of its flank spring the head waters of the Derwent, whose streams, uniting in a deep hollow, flow half round the hill and thence set out on their long journey to the Trent. To carry out our programme punctiliously, we ought to have hunted out the most considerable of the numerous claimants to the title of infant Derwent, and followed every curve and twist downstream. But we were already late for our appointment with the two men from Dunford Bridge. In vain we scanned the seamed and furrowed face of Featherbed Moss across the Derwent yonder. We ran down the rough hill-side to the river. There was no sign of them there. Still they might have been delayed, just as we had, by the exceeding roughness of the way. We would wait a bit and improve the hour by finishing the sandwiches. In the pool beside our resting-place we swilled the mire from our foot-gear. One man left his boots in the river to soak, and they were eventually carried over the waterfall, giving him some trouble to rescue them. Then we started again, hoping the other two travellers were in front.

How many times we crossed from Derbyshire into Yorkshire and back again, I could not say; the gay young stream, recking little of its duty to guard the county boundary, skips playfully from side to side of its wild ravine. Here it tumbles through rocky straits, there flows deep and silent beneath a shaly cliff, now spreads over sand and shingle, and now eddies in a big pool. The slabs at the margin are chiselled into curious patterns, and sometimes a natural bath is cut in the solid rock and polished well nigh as smooth as marble. The sight of one broad pool with a waterfall at the head was irresistible. Four of us had flung our clothes on the heather in a twinkling, and, hot and perspiring as we were, plunged straight into the liquid freshness. Two who were expert divers showed us some amusing antics, or, as the euphuist of the party most elegantly put it, performed some interesting evolutions in the aquatic element.

We were still more than half a score of miles from Bamford, and the missing men had not appeared. We could not afford any more loitering, but pushed on in earnest. Anon the river takes a wide sweep and the narrow clough broadens into a valley. From the shooters' track that runs high above the scarped banks we see a long way up the wild slopes of Howden Moor and Ronksley Moor to left and right. Here, in the wider reaches of the valley, lie a number of great mounds that look remarkably like moraine heaps, though they may possibly be portions of the fell-side detached ages ago by the river, which may afterwards have altered its course. Both the Derwent and the Ashop frequently undermine the shaly hillsides and cause extensive landslips.

And now the trees begin. First come the ashes and birches, growing sparsely and then in sociable groups, and next we enter a woody pass that reminds us of Dovedale, in spite of characteristic differences. There is nothing in Derbyshire more beautiful than this part of the Derwent's progress, in the spring at all events, for it is springtime here, though twenty miles south it is summer. Primroses peep from mossy nooks beneath the hazels and dwarf oaks, there are smooth plots of greensward, while a little way off are the brown ling, the slowly unfurling bracken, and the bilberry bushes with their warmly tinted leaves and delicate pink globes. Boulders and scarps of millstone grit overhang the woods, and waterfalls splash among ferns and mossy rocks. Softest greens and warmest browns in all shades of harmonious combination, and the gleaming river giving life and movement to the scenery. Even the brilliant contrasts of Dovedale can hardly vie with all this mellow beauty. And on either hand are the vastness and deep silence of the moorlands, penetrating the heart with a sense of mystery and awe.

At last we are in sight of Slippery Stones, where the twin brooks come stealing down from the quiet recesses of Bull Clough and Cranberry Clough. Never again shall we see this spot as once it was. Already the engineers are at work making the reservoir, and in due time we shall behold what an artificial loch with landscape gardening can effect to repair the damage done to nature. The valleys soon grow soft and pastoral. At every few miles we advance a week nearer the height of summer. The primroses and violets on the banks have long lost their freshness, in the fields the pale gold of the cowslip is quenched in the fiercer yellow of the buttercups. Beside the lane to Howden Farm, the first habitation we have seen since early morning, the sides of the fields are thickly covered with bluebells—pure masses of blue—and the hawthorn is flowering on the first hedge. We wished there were no train to catch, and that we might stay here and watch the day decline. The euphuist said he would tarry willingly if anybody would bring him some viands. The word stuck; we begged him to hurry on to Ashopton Inn, and order tea and viands for six. At Ouzleden Bridge one member proposed crossing the hills to Edale Station, as shorter than walking down the valley to Bamford. We tried to persuade him that this was a delusion, but he was so convinced that he finally went off alone. Another mile or two and we reached Ashopton, entering the inn through a crowd of tourists, spotlessly attired, who stared in wonderment at our peat-stained and unkempt appearance.

After performing prodigies upon a round of cold beef, we strolled on to Bamford Station, surprised to see nothing of the two adventurers from Dunford Bridge. And where was our sixth man? He was not on the platform at Edale. But the train was kept waiting for some minutes, and presently we saw the station-master at the gate waving his arm wildly to some one in the distance. Then our belated wanderer came rushing in, breathless and perspiring, and tumbled into our carriage as the train moved off. Just as we had opined, in thinking out his route from Ouzleden Bridge he had omitted the important detail that there were two ridges to cross with the Ashop valley between. This made a considerable difference, not merely to the mileage, but to the ups and downs of the walk. He admitted his error with suitable contrition, and in consideration of the good tea we had enjoyed at Ashopton we forgave him.

The fate of the other pair was not ascertained till next day, and then the details of their adventures were carefully shrouded in mystery. We learned, however, that they had failed to reach the Derwent, and had strayed somehow into the valley of the Little Don, where one of them had tumbled into the stream. Eventually they had got to Sheffield, and thence caught a train for home. Owing to the great difficulties experienced by travellers in tracing rivers down from their watersheds, they proposed to memorialise the Royal Geographical Society, with a suggestion that the heads of all streams should be legibly marked with their correct names and other useful facts. In this way, the enterprise of our great advertising firms could be employed to better purpose than in spoiling landscapes with which the public are familiar merely to give unnecessary information.

V.

A RIDGE WALK AND A SCRAMBLE
OR TWO.

IN his " Climbing in the British Isles," Mr. Haskett
Smith says, with reference to the average character
of Derbyshire rock, " When it does offer a climb,
it ends it off abruptly, just as we think the enjoyment
is about to begin." This criticism, which, I trust, will
be made less sweeping in the next edition, does indeed
lie against the half-dozen scrambles to be found by
anyone taking that fine walk along the edges from
Baslow to Higgar Tor and beyond. They are too
insignificant to be more than an addition to the pleasures
of this delightful ramble, which combines the richest
scenery of pastoral Derbyshire with stirring views of
crag and wilderness. We were not come out to-day on
purpose to scramble, but an odd rock or two in our
way never came amiss, nor would we enjoy the scenery,
with its vivid and incessant contrasts, any the less for
such wayside amusement.

We were quickly in the wilderness when we had left
the precincts of Chatsworth House. Strolling through
prim Baslow, we rose a few hundred feet, and the land
of primroses and violets was far behind; we were in
the flowerless clime of the moors. It was one of the
early days in spring, only just on the right side of
winter, and the hollow valley up which the Chesterfield
road wends steeply beside the Barbrook, far into the
moorland solitudes, was still clad in the mellowest russet
tints, as it had been for many a bitter month. And

winter was still alive in the furious blast that met us
on the hill-top. Baslow Edge and Curbar Edge are the
beginnings of the long escarpment, which runs northward almost continuously to Stanage, and flanks the
great breadths of moorland. Their solitudes and
silences, not long ago, inspired William Watson with
a noble sonnet.

> " Change comes not, this dread temple to profane,
>   Where time by æons reckons, not by years.
>   Its patient form one crag, sole stranded, rears,
>   Type of whate'er is destined to remain
>   While yon still host, encamped on night's waste plain,
>   Keep's armèd watch, a million quivering spears."

It was with no feeling of irreverence, though the
sonneteer might have thought us profane, that we used
the "one crag, sole stranded," for a few minutes'
scrambling; at least, I presume that description relates
to the Eagle Stone. This oddly shaped monolith is
deeply weathered along the bedding joints, and a staircase is thus formed, with overhanging instead of
receding steps. Even so, the rock-gymnast finds two,
if not three ways up it, and we get some agreeable
entertainment here, before proceeding on the even
tenour of our way.

Now Froggatt Edge begins, one of the longest walls
of unbroken cliff in the whole district. The height
varies from forty to a hundred feet. From south to
north there is no way from the bottom to the top that
does not involve scrambling of more or less difficulty,
and there are long stretches without a fissure or a ledge
to relieve their sheer blankness. In one place, the
strength of water or frost has hewn out a deep, square
recess, with vertical walls some sixty or seventy feet
high, as smooth as the walls of a slate-quarry. One
side of the recess is deeply fractured, and a narrow

D

fissure zigzags from top to bottom. I tried to climb it once, without success, after a long day's walking and scrambling, and it is still waiting for some hour of excessive energy or some person of exceptional strength of arm. Then for a mile or more we paid all our attention to the view outspread beneath our league-long platform. Save here and there, where you have to pick your way between outcropping slabs of grit, the walking is smooth, and leaves you at leisure to stare about; there are whole furlongs of soft, elastic turf. On the right hand are the bilberry tussocks, the dark brown ling, the fresh green foliage of the crowberry, with the moss-hags between; and then the rugged, uncouth surface of the East Moor stretches away to a gloomy horizon that blends with the stormy sky. On the left are the life and movement of the Derwent valley far below, contrasting with this stern tranquillity. And again there is the contrast between the green meadows, brown fallows, and soft masses of woodland in the valley; and the ruggedness of the crags, the grandeur of edge piled up beyond edge in the distance, right away to cloud-swept Kinder and the Derwent's misty home among the fells. The cliff that we were skirting is cloven and rent into enormous blocks, that are piled up in outstanding rock-towers at one or two points. Through the rents we could see right up the long, gleaming limestone avenue of Middleton Dale. Eyam was on the edge of the brown moors above it, and Calver embosomed in the woody vale beneath. Through the rents, also, we looked down on the Derwent's flashing shallows, whose roaring came up the hill in organ-swells as the wind shifted and blew in gusts; and we looked, too, on the calm, unruffled deeps beyond, filling their stillness with the greens and browns of the wooded hills.

But the silence and lifelessness of the moor are only on the surface. Apart from the continual movement due to the wind, the thunder it made among the crags and the different rustlings of its passage through the different kinds of herbage, there was the frequent cry of birds—whinchats and plovers, redshanks and grouse. It was the matrimonial season with the grouse, and many a dark-plumed moor-cock did we see strutting about in the heather. They were surprisingly—nay, stupidly, tame; and the hares, which had scarcely lost all the white of their winter coats, were in no great hurry to be off, but squatted on their haunches, and stared at us as if we were the first human creatures they had seen this year.

Above the Chequers Inn we found fresh diversion in two scrambles of fair merit. The first was a curious gully or chimney, passing like a gutter right through the escarpment, and undercut so much by the weathering away of shaly rocks at the base that we spent far longer straining to get inside than in climbing to the top. The other was a different affair. On the sloping wall of the crags a deep and narrow slit ran up from a grassy ledge. We had some trouble in reaching the ledge, and it looked shaky; but with a long stride I swung myself on to it, and the mass of earth and roots held firm. Thence to the top it was a hard struggle, friction against gravity, for there were no proper holds, all we got was a pull sideways against the rounded edge of the cleft. It was one of the neatest forty-foot problems we had come across.

We halted at the Chequers, a quaint little inn nestling trustfully under the crags, whose poised boulders and top-heavy pinnacles, most unstable to behold, have spared its humble roof for centuries, as if by a miracle. Then we crossed the hillside to the edge over Grindleford, and took a rough-and-tumble course down to the station through Padley Woods. Near this spot, at an earlier date, a pair of us had bagged another queer little climb, that may as well be described here, in case anyone else would like to add a stone to our miniature cairn. In one of the derelict quarries that are now beautifully overgrown with ferns and shrubs, we found a gritstone pinnacle, about 40ft. high, which had been left as a sort of trophy by the quarrymen. It had smooth vertical sides, and a crown of shattered blocks that actually overhung; but finding one angle thin enough to be gripped with arms and legs, we determined to try this, although the rib of rock on which our weight would depend was separated from the parent stone by fissures that went clean through. Before trusting it, however, we tested its stability as well as we could, and also got the rope round a loose flake weighing several hundredweight, and jerked it off so as to clear a way to the rib. But a judgment fell on us for this barefaced attempt to alter the geography of the country, for in falling the heavy fragment caught the rope and completely severed it. Luckily the rope was not required to get up or down this crazy pinnacle; the doubtful rib held, we swarmed up and over it, shuddering for a moment when we felt it quiver, and in three minutes we were on the top.

The next section of our ridge walk began at Bamford Station. Win Hill was the first summit, and we climbed to it by way of the bleak-looking village of Thornhill, straggling over its south shoulder. Bearing to the right we got on the steep grass slope that runs straight down to the beautiful Derwent, at that part of its course where the moorland stream is transformed to a lowland river. This slope is like a mountain-side in steepness, and also in the boggy nature of the ground.

Photo by   *G.A. Fowkes, Derby.*

THE CRAZY PINNACLE, GRINDLEFORD

THE WINNATS.

It was a tough ascent, but we were out of the wind, and that meant a good deal. Jumping a stone wall, we got on the moors again, and mounting through stubborn heather-stems to the sharp ridge of bare rock that caps the hill so finely, we met the wind once more with a vengeance. If anyone doubts the geological theory as to the erosion of gritstone by the agency of sand driven by the wind, let him face such a sand-blast as that; the sharp grains were like small stones, they stung our faces like tiny arrows. There was no standing upright on the windy crest; so we sought shelter under the lee of the rocks to enjoy our sandwiches and the view. This is a grandly comprehensive one, for Win Hill looks up and down a complex series of dales. Derwent Dale, upstream and downstream, may be counted as two, for it is two to Win Hill, and the sudden change of character has already been alluded to. Ashop Dale is the wildest of all; Edale's spacious curves and mountainous environment are most superb; then come the wide Vale of Hope, and Bradwell Dale, under its overshadowing edges; and between are woody combes like the leafy defile of the Ladybower, and Jagger's Clough. The last winds up from a corner of Edale, between woods of tufted larch and dwarf oak, and steep slopes of brake fern, the very type of a Devonshire combe, till it comes to the bare brown heath, and disappears high up in the mountain of shadows that is Kinder. The dales and the high moors, with their nabs and wickens and black rocky tors, were, notwithstanding, surpassed in grandeur by the extraordinary sky. A storm threatened in the south part of the heavens, and a swollen cloud of darkness shadowed the far head of Ashop Clough, and massed the crags of Fairbrook Naze and the distant fells in a chaos of gloomy shapes. Meanwhile, to east and west, blue

leagues of sky had been swept clean by the wind, and
the sun was shining over dale and hill between.

We ran down the shaggy slopes of heather and
bracken to Hope, where the bridge crosses the Noe, and
then breasted the side of conical Lose Hill. We tried
to find the line of ascent that sheltered us most from
the tremendous wind which still came whistling round
the hill; it had rather strengthened than abated. Lose
Hill is not a contemptible hill to climb, especially after
a long day's beating to windward; and when we arrived
at the curious depression on its peaky top we flung
ourselves down pretty well spent. The view is about
equal to that from Win Hill, and we were to have it,
or something nearly as good, as a companion, all the
way along the narrow ridge to Mam Tor; our prospect
was to include both sides of the ridge and both dales,
save where an unlucky wall gets in the way. To the
right we commanded the whole length and breadth of
Edale, the finest of the Derbyshire dales, to all appearance enclosed by a continuous ring of hills, since the
winding outlet is concealed by the slopes of Lose Hill.

All along the north side of Edale the Scout extends
its southern wall, broken and indented by profound
inlets that wind up among the crags to the storm-swept
plateau. The exquisitely smooth green of the meadows
and pastures in the valley, with their lines and tufts of
woodland, contrasted vividly with all this gloom and
uncouthness. Our ridge narrowed as we approached
Back Tor. Skirting the lofty precipice of disintegrating
shale on the Edale side, we felt it was lucky the wind
did not blow from the opposite quarter, or the passage
would have been exceedingly dangerous. The cliff
looks enticing to the scrambler, but the crumbling rock
makes it useless for sport.

From this height we looked right across the fair vale

of Castleton, and surveyed the great curves of the limestone hills that bound it, their very monotony of sombre
green, almost entirely bare of trees, imparting a certain
grandeur to their rolling contours. The narrow gateway
of Cave Dale, narrow enough indeed to be closed by a
portcullis, and the huge rift at the mouth of Peak
Cavern, were insignificant scars on the broad hillside;
even the pinnacled defile of the Winnats, with beetling
crags of limestone hanging aloft as if to threaten
assailants, looked a very little thing in this great area
of swelling heights. Still we followed the ups and
downs of our ridge, a regular switchback, and now we
were on the long and gentle rise to Mam Tor. We
did not skirt its crumbling precipice too closely, for the
wind swept across the open top with a violence there
was no withstanding. This majestic precipice is as bad
as Back Tor as a climb, yet a friend of mine once
tempted Providence by ascending the slight indentation
in its face, wriggling and squirming like a worm over
its smooth and slippery slopes of shale. He slowly
reached a point just under the crest of steep rock that
runs along the whole cliff. It was the most dangerous
part of the ascent, for the angle here turned against
him, and the holds—if holds you could call them—grew
more rotten and slippery. He lost his hold. What
followed was not exactly a fall and not exactly a sitting
glissade, but something betwixt and between; and he
went something like a hundred feet before he could
stop. He slid, jumping and jolting, over the crumbling
courses of shale, whose rounded edges bumped him
and shoved him further, but spared him any severer
punishment; and when he was landed on his back at
the foot of the cliff he was very little the worse for the
catastrophe. He actually had the assurance, later on,
to make another and a successful attempt to scale this
formidable crag.

Our ridge continues in a curving line round by Lord's Seat, the culmination of Rushup Edge, and by Cowburn to Kinder Scout, thus half encircling the head of Edale. Cowburn, in fact, might be considered as a lofty isthmus connecting the gritstone elevations of the Peak and the Pennine Range with the great limestone tableland of mid-Derbyshire. But for Cowburn, the backbone of England would be dislocated at this point — the tremendous undertaking of tunnelling that hill would not have daunted the early engineers, and the whole railway system of the Midlands would have been simplified. We were tired, and also hungry, the wind having consumed our alimentary fuel at a prodigious rate; so we abandoned the remainder of our ridge walk for the time being, and dropped down to hospitable Castleton. At the back of Mam Tor, where the old and the new roads separate, one to take the long and easy circuit round the flanks of Tray Cliff, the other to rush violently down the steep place of the Winnats, is Windy Knoll— and it is properly named. There the gale seemed to be in a terrible fury, and not quite sure what it would be at, for it seemed to be leaping at us from every quarter in succession, and trying fair means and foul to fling us off our balance. But inside the " Wind Gates " there is always a steady draught, either up or down, and to-day it was coming up like a tide-race, virtually cancelling the break-neck steepness of the road, so that we could run downhill at top speed without making any great pace. There are not many good climbs in the Winnats Pass; there seldom are any on mountain limestone, and we were not tempted to dawdle. The defile has a wild and romantic look, especially if seen from the heights on either side, and old romancers, like Mrs. Linnæus Banks, were fond of making it a scene for tragic episodes. Readers of

Joseph Hatton's " Banishment of Jessop Blythe," also, will remember the murder perpetrated here, on which hinges the plot of that Castleton novel.

I may as well describe the continuation of our ridge walk, as it was completed later. From the point where we quitted the ridge, the going steadily grew worse and worse. The tops of these hills are partly grassy and heathery in part, and always disagreeably inclined to be boggy; big tussocks of herbage, cushions of coarse grass with a hard lump inside, cover the ground, with deep ruts and pitfalls between—your foot never knows whether it is coming on something solid or going to plunge into a slimy hole. On the right, Cowburn and Lord's Seat break away suddenly towards Edale, in long, clean slopes of nearly a thousand feet, straight and unfurrowed but for one or two stony cloughs that cut deeply in near Dale Head. Cowburn's sky-line is more level even than the top of Kinder, and far less interesting; such monotonous flatness seems unnatural at this elevation. Beneath us extends the long ridge that we traversed from Lose Hill to Mam Tor, a sort of Striding Edge. First we have the lofty, sweeping sides of Lord's Seat, and the cliffs and rugged dome of Mam Tor; then Back Tor seems to cut the ridge in two with its sudden wall; and beyond, in misty outline, come the peaky tops between it and Lose Hill, with the vague form of Win Hill in the distance, seemingly a shadow of the last summit cast across the valley. But we are tired of these exasperating tussocks and the dreary level; we seem hardly any nearer yet to Kinder Scout. There it lies, a confusion of blue and dark brown shadows, all indistinctness, save where vagrant gleams flit across the haze. Yet always the stark, swart shapes of Crowden Tower, Noe Stool, and the rest of those bizarre clumps and tors of gritstone, stand out clear from the shadows above the springs of Noe.

Many deep trenches, big enough to hold a good-sized river, wind across the flatness; they are quite dry, and give one a striking idea of the difference a week of rain would make in the water supply. And now Edale and the eastern acclivities have slipped out of view, but the valleys and hills to the west have not appeared above the drear horizon; yet we are descending perceptibly. Anon we come to a scarped hollow, where a couple of brooks meet and beget the main stream of Roych Clough. But the brooks will not slake our thirst to-day; the streams have been extinct for a long while, all but an odd basin or two of green and slimy water that lie among the slabs. Yet the dingles through which they wind are delightfully fresh, with their ferny and heathery brake sheltering scores of grouse, larks, plovers, and other birds, that fly up at our approach with a startling whirr. Now the bold height of South Head crops up in front above the dull monotony of heath and bog, and down Roych Clough we catch a glimpse of wooded dingles and lines of green fields, where the bare hills slope into the pleasant vale of Chapel-en-le-Frith. At the back of the spacious valley is a lofty tableland, a great square shadow against the hazy sky, with abrupt ends and a sky-line like a stone wall. This is the north edge of Comb's Moss; and in the valley, almost touched by its shade, is a gleaming sheet of water, the Comb's Moss Reservoir: a lake is so much out of keeping with the prevalent features of Peak scenery, that the shimmering phantom hardly seems real.

Our ridge gradually narrowed, and we commanded another view. That on the left was soft and smiling, full of comfort and good cheer; the northward prospect was vast, shadowy, and inhospitable. There lay the great hollow, full of lesser heights and hollows, between

Mount Famine and the western edge of Kinder, a land
of bare hills and moors and deep green valleys, with
a solitary farm nestling at the bottom of Dimpus
Clough. The blue boundaries of this desolate valley
died away among the misty fells to the north, and soon
we lost sight of them altogether, as other ranges came
shouldering up in front. Clambering to the top of
South Head, heedless of keepers and walls, for the sake
of its excellent view, we dropped again to the saddle
between it and the hill of the hungry name, and followed
the deep upland valley down to Chinley, erstwhile an
insignificant cluster of houses, now one of the busiest
junctions on the Midland Railway, and soon perhaps
to be another of Manchester's ring of suburbs. We are
a long while yet ridding ourselves of the companionship
of the hills; noble contours still crowd around us—
Eccles Pike, Cracken Edge, Chinley Churn. And
though the clearness of the sky is sullied with foul
smoke-clouds from the border towns of Cheshire and
Lancashire, even the spread of ignoble villages and
factories, that settle in the dales and climb the ridges,
cannot obliterate or obscure the grand old shapes—the
same now as they were when the land was a wilderness,
and as they will be when it is a wilderness again. The
very place-names have the same savour of romance and
antiquity, that the philologist relishes with so much gusto
in such moorland names as Fairbrook Naze, Ladybower,
Wildboar Clough, Ouzleden, and Featherbed Moss.
Throstle Bank, Dimpus, the Roych, Ollerenshaw, Black
Edge are just as full of suggestion and romantic sound.
To pick them out on the map is, to a lover of old
picturesque words, like finding plums in a pudding.
And such names are not found amid commonplace
landscapes; they reflect the original wildness and
the indestructible beauty, as well as a little of the
history of the country-side they belong to.

VI.

BY WAY OF DANE CLOUGH TO LUDCHURCH.

HALF-WAY from Buxton to Axe Edge we walked into a fog; thick curtains of fog were unfurled around us when we sat down for a smoke at the cairn. Speaking without prejudice, I should say that I never found the summit of Axe Edge half so fine a place before. Under ordinary conditions this is a most disappointing climb. After taking the trouble to ascend to the height of 1,804 feet above sea-level you expect to behold something unusual; but what is it that you see? Around are humpy tablelands only a few dozen feet lower than you, which make it almost impossible to persuade yourself that you are on a lofty hill. Not far away, nearly as high as the cairn, you see a house or two, as ugly as if cut in lengths off a street in the Black Country; and, at a greater distance, that unpicturesque edifice, the Cat and Fiddle. Several roads are a little way off, then come a few slopes of railway, and mile upon mile of hideous, blasted country, which the lime-burners have turned into something more squalid than a desert. To be sure, there are grand sights in the distance, but these are comparatively insignificant in the total view, and you gladly seek a lower level to lose sight of the greater blemishes.

But now we have about us all the proper insignia of the royallest hill-top. We might be on Ingleborough, Crossfell, or even Helvellyn. There is the grey cairn, built to weather a thousand storms; the peat-moss is at our feet; the brown pools, the rocks, the ling; there is the wonted garniture of empty bottles, string, and sandwich papers. Physical experience tells us that we are eighteen hundred feet above the sea; yonder, we know that, were it clear enough, we might see a mountain top in Wales; and in another quarter we believe that there is nothing but air and cloud between us and the Irish Sea. In comparison with which far flight, merely a stone's throw away, we can almost see the Scout marshalling his long lines of swarthy cliff, and the edges and moors extending in confused array far into the wilds of Yorkshire.

There is another privilege connected with the fog, it enables you to get lost. Axe Edge in a mist is no commonplace hill. We take advantage of the last privilege forthwith. Compass and map in hand, two of us—there are eight in all—lay down an imaginary line for the head of Dane Clough. Over heather, turf, and bog we go, without deviating an inch, so we imagine, from the bearings indicated by the Ordnance Survey; and when, it would seem, we must have over-walked our goal at least a mile, we unexpectedly find ourselves on a road, looking at a finger-post that tells us we are making tracks rapidly for Macclesfield, a place we have no more desire to reach just now than we have to see Manchester or Oldham. A valuable half-hour had been lost when, at length, we came to the bight in the uplands where the little River Dane begins to hew its rugged way down to Love Lane Bridge. The defile it has fashioned for itself is as grand as that of the Fairbrook, or even the Kinder river on the Scout, save for one thing lacking, the sheer gritstone edge at the top. Here the rocks are shaly; and while great sweeping slopes are formed on each side of the river, there are few abrupt crags, and few of those big boulders thwarting the current and filling the clough with cascades. Heather and bents and lush mosses cover the banks and make the footing treacherous, whether we scramble along the steep fell-side or wade the marshes beside the stream.

Some distance down the clough there is a huge quarry, enveloping both sides of the gorge with enormous rubbish heaps. Quarries, as a rule, are unbeautiful objects, but in this one it was impossible to deny a certain primitive grandeur. The sun was striving to dispel the mists, which were changed for a while into luminous sheets, deepening the aerial perspective. The piles of hewn rock, and the immense heaps of shale, with the stream painfully cleaving through, looked like a giant's assault upon nature. Still the Dane flows on and on between the curves and scarps of the hillside, in its precipitous ravine. The walking was extremely rough, and we thought it might save time and trouble if we quitted the clough and followed the crest of a high spit of land to our left. One man obstinately kept to the stream's uneasy track, and whilst, with our usual bad luck, we got adrift again, he managed to reach the trysting place before us. We blundered on, unable to make out any decisive landmark in the haze that magnified hill and dale to a cloudy vastness. Cut-thorn Hill (1,500ft.), which we mistook for Shutling's Low, looked an imposing peak, spiring up from the bottom of the clough, a shapely cone. But the most distinct recollection of the morning's wanderings is associated with a lonely cottage, where we desired to ask information and were forbidden all access by a fierce and horrible-looking tyke. When the gentle beast had barked himself hoarse, and nearly burst his chain in trying to get at us, his master, a little less uncouth, came and mollified him with a thick stick, assuring us that he was perfectly harmless, it was only his play. This out-of-the-way corner of England, this "no man's land" on the boundary of three counties, was a lawless region to a surprisingly recent date, and blood-curdling are some of the legends belonging to it. Everybody has heard of "flash coin," which used to be one of the exports from Flash, the village on the misty hill yonder; and the legend of the prize-fighters who used to step from Cheshire into Derbyshire, and from Derbyshire into Staffordshire, when the county police arrived, is, on the face of it, true. Even now the sparse inhabitants seem to have a look of savagery about them, quite in keeping with the scenery. When we got down at last to Gradbach, a straggling village at the confluence of several deep glens, we had wasted more time than we felt comfortable about, and we took precautions not to miss our way through the woods to Ludchurch. For two hours or so we had been coming downhill, now we began to ascend. If you have seen Killiecrankie Pass or the Findhorn Glen or the Pass of Leny, you will have an idea of the noble valley cut by the Dane and its tributary waters through this high frontier range into Cheshire. It is not equal to those celebrated scenes, of course, but it is comparable. Woods upon woods, a veritable precipice of trees, rise to the sky-line on either hand, and the rift between is so narrow that you see nothing below you but cloud beyond cloud of foliage, from the depths of which, seemingly unfathomable, the noise of the river comes floating up in bursts of music.

As we pursue our forest path, we catch a glimpse suddenly of strange gritstone shapes sitting like giants at parley, on a ledge far up among the wooded heights. Is it Ludchurch? we ask ourselves. What a romantic portal, and what imposing warders! But it is not Ludchurch yet; only the Castle Rocks, a group of crags tottering on the edge of the leafy precipice, and commanding an ample view of the woods and the pass. A turning brings us to the entrance of the weird chasm

we have come all these miles to see. The region of
the limestone and the grit is prolific in natural curios,
from pot-holes and bottomless pits to Robin Hood's
Strides and Twelve Apostles, but of all such marvels
the most singular is surely Ludchurch. It is not merely
a waterless ravine—those are common in the Peak—it
is a ravine that, obviously, no stream has had anything
to do with. A winding cleft in the hill-side, nearly a
hundred feet deep, a long jump in width, and some
two hundred yards in length, with a floor that does
not slope from end to end, but simply goes up and
down without any apparent cause or purpose—it is a
puzzle indeed for anyone not acquainted with the freaks
played by the grit at Brimham or Roach End. It is
merely an example, on a biggish scale, of a common
trick of the gritstone; there has been a rock slide, in
which a long slice of the hill crest has started forward
bodily for a few feet, and left this yawning gap as a
theme for mythologising rustics.

Who was Lud? and why is this his church? Bladud,
his reputed son, we are well acquainted with, that king
of Britain who cuts such a comical figure in legend,
bathing with his leprous pigs in the marshes of Aquæ
Solis, and winning renown as a sort of Esculapius, to
be perpetuated in a grinning statue over one of the hot
baths of Bath. Lud, however, has associations of a
different colour attaching to his name, few and vague
though they be.

We had brought an Alpine rope, expecting to enjoy
some scrambling on the walls of the gorge and on the
Castle Rocks. But the wet fog had drenched the rocks
with moisture, the walls were reeking and slimy, water
dripping from overhanging ledges as in a cave. The
place is indeed much like a cave with the roof off. A
few of us clambered up to the niche wherein the figure-
head of the good ship " Swythamley," named after the

Photo by   *Rd. Keene, Limited.*

LUDCHURCH.

domain of which this is part, was placed as a memorial after she was wrecked. This shrine of Our Lady of Lud must be sadly in need of cleansing, to judge by the state of their garments when they came down. Meanwhile I went up to the heathery slope above the fissure, and looked from the top into the curious abyss. The grit all round is cracked and rifted with the same convulsion that produced the ravine, yet it is with frightful suddenness that one comes to the brink, half hidden as it is with birch, ash, and rank heather. Has the thing ever served as a death-trap for an ignorant foe? Its absolute perfection for such a purpose almost convinces one that it has a tragic history. But the most thrilling incident I can discover, besides the unauthenticated legends about Sir Walter de Lud-Auk and the fair maiden who sacrificed herself to save the Lollards at their worship in Ludchurch, is the one that befel Squire Trafford of Swythamley, whose horse carried him almost into the ravine, and left him bestriding it in a perilous situation until he was rescued.

But it was high time for us to decide whether we were to go ahead, and climb the Roaches, or spend the waning afternoon here. We made up our minds that to venture on the misty hills was to lose the last train home; we had been befogged too much already.

So we scrambled all over the Castle Crags for an hour, performing all the regulation exercises of the Alpinist fraternity; and then trudged up that disheartening three miles from Gradbach to Flash, the putative highest village in England, where we had tea, the supply of eggs being renewed by accommodating hens whilst we ate the first dozen. Hence by way of Flash Bar and the wells of Dove to Buxton, which seemed a place of portentous culture and civilisation after this day's ramble in its barbarous environs.

E

VII.

OVER CHESHIRE INTO YORKSHIRE.

A RAMBLE through the uncleansed streets of Sheffield in the early dawn is an incongruous prelude to a day on the moors. We had left town by the Midland at a dark and inclement hour of what the policeman calls the morning, and we found that the Great Central would not take us on to Crowden for two hours. So we fed our minds with the most abysmal contrasts imaginable to the spaciousness and purity of earth, air, and sky that we were to enjoy presently, sucking what satisfaction we might from the smoky presages of a fine day coming. For a while, however, even this confidence was shaken, for it seemed that the weather on the far side of the Pennine crest was of a different colour from that to the east. Out of Woodhead tunnel we plunged into a seething tumult of steam and mist, how much was from the engine and how much from the stormy fells we could not see, for all alike was white, dank, and violently agitated. But the face of things was changed completely when we came out again after breakfast, having crossed the bridge from Derbyshire into Cheshire. The mists were breaking along the tops of the wild hills, the sun shone warm for September, and windows of lustrous blue were opening among the cloud-wrack.

We were going to explore new ground, a corner of Cheshire, wedged in between Yorkshire and Derbyshire, that is unknown to the guide-books and undiscovered by the tourist. We had been attracted by the emptiness of the Ordnance map at this particular spot—an emptiness that experience taught us to fill with the unrifled scenery of crag and waterfall and solitary fell. Not a dot was there to indicate railway or road, houses or anything human; nothing but whorls of contour-lines, flanked by close parallels that marked deep and precipitous valleys. Among these we had chosen the deep clough of Crowden Great Brook as a suitable entrance to the unknown territory, and it proved a lucky shot.

Leaving homely little Crowden behind and passing the uppermost reservoirs of the Manchester waterworks, we came to a series of rifle-ranges on the margin of the wilderness, and spent a few minutes looking at the mechanism of the targets. But we were not sorry to turn our backs on these last vestiges of the dull and tedious world, and to feel that for half a day at least we were to enjoy the perfection of solitude. As yet the culminating hill-crest that shuts out Yorkshire was far out of sight, and the next house we were to set eyes on was far beyond that barrier. The dale grew deeper and wider as we got among the high fells. Bareholme Moor heaved itself higher and higher on our right, a sloping expanse of brake, heather, and bilberry; many-coloured, brown and dusky green, bright russet and purplish-black, with grey old rocks crowning the hillside and jutting through the shaggy ground. On the other side, the mighty retaining-wall of Featherbed Moss was split and rent into craggy spurs and savage cloughs by the descending streams. Rakes Rocks tempted us with the offer of some pretty climbing, but we resisted the appeal, for a much finer cliff edged the next hill-top, and even a mile away two straight black chimneys promised good sport. Our track now began to mount the rugged hillside in the direction of this towering wall of millstone grit.   The sun was hot at our backs, though the wind in front chilled our perspiring breasts; and when we dipped into Oaken Clough, crossing the water-worn slabs of the stream-bed, we gladly sat down to rest beside a plashing waterfall, above a pellucid basin that almost seduced us to stay and bathe.

We had reached a point whence we could survey both our onward path and the journey we had come.   Around us cliff-crested slopes, rocky gorges where the streams cut through the edges, and the vast trench of the valley, with the deeper trench of the brook within it, were all drawn in the grand primitive lines of nature.   Curve after curve of the moorlands rose in front into clear sky; but whether the visible horizon was the summit we were to cross, it was impossible to tell at present.   Two miles ahead, in the middle of the valley, a black gritstone tor sprang aloft into two peaks.   When first it emerged, its lofty, trenchant form seemed to dominate everything; but as our point of view was lifted, it sank relatively to the surrounding hills, and presently we were to look right down on its squat insignificance.   Many things on the moors look biggest and most imposing at a distance.   A diaphanous haze, like a thin blue smoke, filled the void between our fell and the great slope over against us, softening the sharp edges of boulder and crag, melting colour into colour, and, as it were, blending the terrestrial prospect with the infinite sky. Farther down the dale, the faded green of the bracken and the russet of last year's witherings, with the weather-toned and lichened blocks of ancient stone, solemn harmonies of mellow and infinitely modulated tints, were suddenly infringed upon by the harsh green of the meadows, which in turn died away among the mists beyond Crowden.

Though the cold, dense mists of early morning had
fled away up the cloughs and vanished hours ago, the
wind coming down our dale was still driving impalpable
veils of haze, like shreds of gossamer, strewing them
in cobwebby films over the high range of moors towards
Bleaklow, and scattering them through the depths of
Longdendale. In the midst of the sunlit haze those
lofty, mountainous shapes were but a duskiness, a
shadow dimly seen, as if the heart of the mist had
condensed to something a little less unsubstantial; all
was vague and nebulous; fells and mists, drenched with
sunlight, were heaped up together against the southern
sky.

Laddow Rocks were grander in reality than they had
looked in the distance. They formed a sheer precipice
of 150ft., at the top of an abrupt and craggy slope.
My friend was no climber, and preferred to rest at the
top while I made a brief exploration of the cliffs. The
first thing was to reach the bottom. I thought I saw
an easy way down near the middle, where a shallow
gully was rather unpleasantly full of *débris*. It proved
more dangerous than easy. Close beside it, a big
tower of gritstone stood out from the cliff, and sent a
steep buttress plunging down more than a hundred feet
to the foot of the rocks. A notch, some 20ft. deep,
sundered it from the main cliff, on which side it had an
overhanging wall that hardly looked a possible climb.
Nevertheless, I thought I might as well try it. So,
planting my feet against the cliff and my hands against
the tower, I managed to walk up the gap till a cornice
came within reach, when I pulled myself over. In
another moment I was on the top. So far so good, but
getting back was a different matter altogether. When
I tried to repeat the manœuvre backwards, my foot fell
short of the cliff by some ten inches. To climb back

by the wall of the pinnacle looked an insane undertaking, for the wind was blowing great guns, and instead of landing in the notch, I should more likely have rolled down the gully to the right or to the left. Seeing my predicament, my companion descended to a point just above the notch, but could see no other way out of the difficulty but a jump across the gap on to a sloping and shaky-looking ledge on the cliff, about six feet away. The distance was nothing, and the take-off excellent, but the penalty of a slip was too bad to think of. He tested the one shred of hand-hold that disclosed itself; he was too precariously fixed himself to render any help. Then, cutting hesitation short, I took the leap, clutched the little corner, and was safe.

Now I continued my way down the gully, which proved more awkward than I anticipated, for there were loose earth and loose splinters about. But creeping round the big buttress to look at the other gully, I found that even worse, so I made the best of my way down the slippery rocks, resigning myself to the inevitable deluge of gritty earth and sand from the choked-up ledges. These nondescript scrambles are often far worse than a difficult but straightforward climb. Safe at the bottom, I surveyed with admiration the huge limb that the rock-tower sends down between the two gullies, and determined to come again some day, with a party properly equipped, and try a fall with such a worthy adversary. The whole range of crags was full of climbing possibilities. Towards the north, they were more solid and massive, the cracks and fissures very straight and rectangular, and for the most part not spoilt by objectionable herbage. I scrambled about the face, and came, at length, to the two steep chimneys that had taken our fancy from afar. They were all but perpendicular, but the goodness of the rock and the abundance of chock-stones made them perfectly feasible. One could track a possible climb for near a hundred feet up; in fact, I was emboldened to ascend half that distance, but the outlet above looked too doubtful for a solitary climber, so I scrambled back; I had been in a parlous situation once already to-day, and my patient friend up aloft must have been getting uneasy at my absence. Scrambling up a detached leaf of rock at the end of the cliff, I rejoined him, and we turned away from the valley towards the gentle slope of Blackchew Head (1,774ft.).

The character of our surroundings was now utterly changed. The area of the valleys is but a small part of these broad moorland tracts. Our eyes roved unimpeded from the borders of Yorkshire, over Lancashire fells and Cheshire fells, to the lofty sky-line of Derbyshire, oblivious of the sundering gulf of Longdendale. It seemed but a level walk from Featherbed Moss to the moors about Glossop. Not a wall, nor a road, not even a shooting butt, over leagues of dusky moorland, broke the majestic curves of uninterrupted space. It was hard indeed to realise that a few hours' walking would take us into the almost interminable streets of Oldham and the towns linked on to it; that we were, in fact, all but encircled by a black manufacturing country and the thickest population in the world.

Rather than prolong the weary trudge through the heather and bilberry, along the summit level of Owl's Head, Round Hill, and Green Hill, to the highest crest of all, Black Hill, we took a short cut across the outskirts of Sliddens Moss. The way was plain before us, we could see every bit of it, but we should have been puzzled to estimate the distance within a mile, so difficult is it to measure vast empty spaces where the eye has nothing definite to rest upon. We allowed ourselves an hour, and were not very much behindhand at the finish. We now drew nigh the spot where the Crowden Water tumbles from the upper level of the moors into the deep valley, and at the mouth of a small tributary we sat down to eat our lunch. Though the water was clear and unstained, it had a most unpalatable twang of peat. For a mile or more we kept crossing and re-crossing the now diminished stream, then we left it, and mounted more perceptibly over tussocky ground, overlaid in many places with the withered foliage of the cloudberry. This part of our walk reminded one of the dreary nakedness of Dartmoor. The heather and the bilberry were getting sparse, there was hardly a sign of animal life, we had not heard the barking cry of the grouse for some time. Suddenly, an enormous host of birds, lapwings or fieldfares, rose up in thousands upon thousands, on the horizon of Black Hill. They sprang up at first like a dense black cloud of smoke, then the edges thinned, and the whole flight opened out like a fan, and wheeled across the sky. They manœuvred in a series of swift formations as they passed over a wide circuit of the moor, marshalling in columns, forming immense squares, flying out in far-stretching crescents. And ever as they massed their columns or scattered over a wider area, the colour of the clouds changed from black to grey, until they melted into the dull sky over Yorkshire.

We crossed the sombre sides of Dun Hill, and now we were nearing the far-extended flat top of Black Hill (1,909ft.), which was roughened at the point we were making for by a curious succession of notches and hillocks. We soon learned what these meant. They were the furrows and ridges, seen end on, of a great peat-moss, resembling those on top of Bleaklow Head and Kinder Scout. When we reached the centre of it all, and stood on the peat-built cairn, the scene around us was one of unmitigated gloom. As far as we could see, there was no end to the mounds of bare, black earth, the slimy gullies, the quagmires and their dismal pools of water and mud. My companion, who had hardly yet acquired a taste for merely stern and desolate scenery, was oppressed with the sheer ghastliness of the place, and was anxious to get away as soon as possible from the prodigious " muck heap," as he called it. And, truly, the idea of being there alone in a mist might well give one the horrors. Even on a clear day there was absolutely nothing to be seen that could be used as a landmark, and we steered ourselves by the compass for the best part of a mile before the grey shadows of a distant hill raised itself above the dreary horizon. Then the ground began to fall away, and, just where we were looking for it, there appeared the glaring white line of the highway, still remote, crossing the waste between Greenfield and Holmfirth, and beside it a bleak little gathering of houses, one of which, we knew, must be the Isle of Skye. The high-sounding name of this Yorkshire hostelry had determined us not to miss it on any account. Our way was all plain sailing now, for the four or five miles to Holmfirth were on the road, and—we thanked our stars for it—all down-hill. Toil and pleasure were nearly over, and we were so drowsy after our early start, that we lay in the heather half-way to the Isle of Skye, and enjoyed a snooze in spite of the churlish wind.

VIII.

A BOXING-DAY ON KINDER SCOUT.

FROM streets sodden with rain and thaw the train took us through dales all white, and presently shot into a whirling snowstorm. Three inches of snow covered dingy Hayfield, but it was melting. As soon, however, as we had left the little town behind and begun to ascend the deep Kinder valley, snow, frost, and fog once more asserted their rights. The white hillsides, broken by the brown cliffs of the quarries and by steep plantations of dwarf oak and fir that mingled their snowy boughs softly with the mist, might have been the bases of Alps, for they rose and rose into cloud far beyond where the eye could follow. A long, sandy Scot, leaning on a gate-post, who scanned our party with an air that we took for admiration of our dauntless bearing towards the perils ahead, turned out to be a keeper, who did not mean to let us hazard ourselves in the wilderness without proper credentials. Having examined our permit, he began to draw an unattractive sketch of the condition of things on the Scout; and, as his countrymen are wont with the Englishman in search of the picturesque, he reasoned with us more in pity than in scorn of our folly. Finding us unappalled, however, he finished up with a warning that we must keep away from the rocks, which were dangerous. We did not tell him that a length of Alpine Club rope was coiled in the rücksack, and that we meant to get as close as we could to the rocks. His belief that we were not quite right in our minds showed itself sufficiently.

As we rose the snow deepened and the mist grew denser. We got astray even before reaching Upper Farm, the lonely homestead where Mrs. Humphry Ward meditated the "History of David Grieve," and its eloquent descriptions of the great fell we were bound for. Here another sentinel was on the look-out for pleasure parties—a cold and unexciting office this wintry day. Henceforward progress was maintained rather by faith than by sight. The only tracks were the not careless ones of a few stray sheep, the solitary footsteps of the postman had ceased, and our prospect was limited to a narrow radius of spotless snow merging into an atmosphere of hueless vapour. The post of fugleman was not without its burdens, for he had to determine a route, beat down a path for those behind him through deep snow, and at the same time sustain with equable face, or rather equable back, a steady fire of snowballs from the jocund rear. The steep hillside drove us presently to seek less slippery footing in the bed of the narrow clough or ravine cut by the Kinder stream. Here there is bog in abundance, and through the still deeper snow our legs sometimes plunged into watery holes, while our toils were varied a little by an occasional tract of boulders, that had to be scrambled over and swept of their snow in the process by our struggling limbs. For the greater part of the way uphill the stream was our guide, but in the higher regions it was ice-bound, and a heavy silence reigned where at other seasons a hundred rills join their voices to the louder one of the brook. An ominous shadow fell upon the wan landscape, as though a thundercloud were brooding over the mist; and we began to doubt as to our where-abouts when, as we approached the crest of the great hill, we listened in vain for the wonted cry of the Downfall, which ought to have been flinging its waters over the cliff not far away. Presently the course of the stream, which had been lost in the folded snow-wreaths, once more showed itself unmistakably in the huge staircase of boulders in the ravine below the fall. The crags also began to loom through the cloudy air from the rugged fell-side to right and left. To avoid the boulders, which were glazed with ice wherever the snow had not buried them, we endeavoured to traverse these slopes, but very quickly came sliding again to the lower level. We crawled and scrambled, we floundered among the boulders, and laboured often desperately to surmount a slippery stone a few feet high; and sure as ever a man opened his lips to speak he trod in a hole or came sliding back over an ice-coated rock.

All this was enjoyable, exhilarating, but it grew monotonous after a while. Then of a sudden our toils were lightened by the appearance of the Downfall a few yards in front, frozen completely, a piece of fairy architecture lovelier far than the finest ice-palace ever dreamed of. Two huge icicles, great in girth as the greatest of Norman piers, fluted and carved fantastically, buttressed the shining façade; the horizontal ledges of the crags were adorned with traceries wrought into curious arcades or fringed with lacework of pendulous ice. A greenish light, a luminous sea-green, irradiated the fabric, distorting the flotsam caught in the ice, and making beautiful the very dirt of the stream viewed through this strange kaleidoscope. While we gazed the sun dissolved the mist, shedding a roseate glow on the pure slopes and the towering pinnacles of snow-slashed gritstone that crown the contiguous cliffs, and flashing in splendour on a slab of ice or ice-bound rock, set in the midst of the frozen waterfall, till it shone again

Photo by

W. Meakin, Newthorpe, Notts.

AT THE FOOT OF KINDER DOWNFALL IN WINTER.

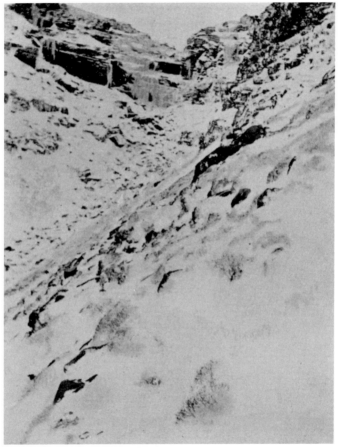

Photo by   *G.A. Fowkes, Derby.*

KINDER DOWNFALL IN WINTER.

like a sheet of precious spar or opal. The photographer,
who had been congratulating himself on not having
lugged the camera through all this snow and fog,
pulled another face when he saw such a masterpiece of
atmospheric effect waxing and waning before his eyes.
Like the angler, he will be able to boast of the fine fish
he has lost. Right inside the fall, with the two great
ice-columns in front, stalactites of ice overhead, and
rudimentary stalagmites on the floor, was a cave; here
we sat to lunch, and here the penitent photographer took
out a little oil-stove from the bag where the camera
should have been, and, melting down some pieces of
ice, boiled bovril for the party. We were just finishing
lunch with a quiet smoke when we heard, or thought
we heard, a shout. Anon a voice replied to our
answering shouts, and thereupon we saw a party of four
climbers toiling up the clough. They were men from
Manchester who had come across the moors from
Glossop; and though they carried a rope, it appeared
they also had found rock-climbing to be out of the
question under such conditions as prevailed up here.
We parted after a friendly colloquy, they to descend
to Hayfield, we to climb the Edge and make our way
across the wide tableland to Edale, where our dinner
was situated.

The next step was to find a way up to the Edge.
Skirting the cliffs we came in a few yards to a breach
in the defences. Here a precipitous slope was crossed
in two places by irregular terraces of rock. So
precarious was the footing on this smooth, snow-clad
slope that we had to crawl along with the utmost caution,
stretched on our sides, and moving in a curious attitude,
hands aiding feet. Just below a shallow gully, falling
bodies—snow perhaps, or stones—had hollowed and
polished a snow-shoot or couloir, that invited us to

take a flying journey to the Kinder stream far below in the mist. Getting across this obstacle was a ticklish feat. At the first terrace three men began scrambling up a corner between two rock-faces, while two others crept out on a ledge to what appeared an easier fissure. This proved hard enough, however, chiefly because the start had to be made with one foot planted on a mass of soft snow that was yielding and slippery. Above the minor cliff came a section of steep hillside. The ten inches of soft, dry snow afforded little foothold, and the hard soil beneath was impenetrable. Only by dint of thrusting arms and feet deep into the snow, then wriggling up by inches, could we make safe progress up to the final barrier. And now we were so cold, coated with ice and snow from head to foot, our extremities congealed, and our fingers senseless and incapable of holding anything, that we found a few yards of nearly vertical rock a severe trial. Our comrades, too, were in difficulties; somewhere away in the mist we could hear them calling for the rope. All the hand-hold the leader could get was by resting with arm and breast on a narrow ledge, and so by glueing his body to the rock he propelled himself awkwardly over the edge of the terrace. Then, as soon as his hands thawed sufficiently, he took the rope out of the rücksack and gave the next man a friendly pull up. Shall we ever get warm again? we thought, as we stamped about on a wind-swept pavement of gritstone. But there was a bit of warm work awaiting us. Following the shout of distress, we found the three others at the foot of a beetling crag which had cut them off. There was nothing to be done but let down the rope and haul them up one by one, in the same fashion as we hauled up their impedimenta; and this was done with no mishap, except that one got hung, Prometheus-

like, for some minutes through the rope's hitching in
a cleft. One by one, with glowing faces, they came
gracefully over the edge, and were carefully deposited
in a safe place. Then, with a brief halt in the stinging
wind, we prepared to cross the plateau to the point
where the Grindsbrook cuts deeply in from Edale, and
narrows the breadth of the tableland to two or three
miles.

Always on Kinder Scout, even in fine weather, the
compass is a desideratum, on account of the general
flatness and the complete absence of landmarks. So
the mere addition of mist to the difficulties of crossing
might seem a trifle. But we found that the combination
of mist and deep snow made it doubtful whether we
should reach the other Edge at all before evening fell.
For half a mile we had the irregular trench of the
Kinder stream for a guide. The brook was frozen,
and we went through into the water only at occasional
spots. But it was hard work—so hard plodding
through the heavy stuff that we tried the adjacent bog
several times, only to find the irregularities and the
innumerable snow-traps still more baffling. A few
grouse darted down the wind from time to time with a
whirr, and we saw the holes in the snow where they
had been roosting, as well as the holes, neatly carved
in the ice, where they drank. What they found to eat
was a mystery, for the only signs of vegetation were
the withered tops of the heather that at every few yards
made a stain on the surface of the snow. These, by the
by, were useful to us as marks of direction—were, in
fact, the only means we had of producing the imaginary
line determined by the compass. One other living
creature we found amid the glacial solitude, a tiny
shrew-mouse, about as big as a filbert, who, I suppose,
ought to have been hibernating. He ran up my

shoulder, and nestled inside my shirt collar, whence I rescued the poor little waif and transported him to the warm paradise of the inn garden at Edale, where, I trust, he fell into the jaws of no bloodthirsty cat.

Presently we had left behind us our guide, the Kinder Water, and were fairly launched on the bewildering maze of heights and hollows, of moss-hags and groughs that in summer, with much mud and very little water, wind perplexingly over the bog. Now at every few steps we plunged into hidden holes, often up to our shoulders, for to pick out solid ground was quite impossible. Once or twice a glint of blue sky shone vaguely through the restless haze, and a reflected gleam from the setting sun coming from the north bewildered us for a while as to our bearings. Soon the air thickened again, wildly distorting visible objects, so that many times we thought we beheld at some distance the channel of the Grindsbrook, broad and deep, and then, proceeding a few steps, found the mist had magnified a little ditch and turned a snow-laden bank into a cliff. Darkness was at hand, and there was no sign of the Edge or of any definite failing in the general flatness. Had we missed the stream and gone off along one of the broad forelands that run out to east and west of the clough? A member of the party showed signs of exhaustion and had to lie down in the snow for a few minutes. Then, a hundred yards or so further, all in a moment, a wide chasm disclosed itself right under the leader's nose; it was the Grindsbrook at last, and gleefully we scrambled down the craggy sides, and began dropping ourselves from ledge to ledge of the half-frozen cascades that descend through a ragged cleft in the gritstone edge into the capacious hollow of Grindsbrook Clough. What recked we now though each slide shot us through the thin crust into a chilly pool, though our legs were

Photo by　　　　　　　　　　　　　　　　　　　　　　*Rd. Keene, Limited.*

ON THE KINDER STREAM BELOW THE DOWNFALL.

wet and icy and our frozen clothes clanked stiff as armour? A big fire and a big rib of beef were smoking for us below there, although somebody did whisper that this might after all be Jagger's or even Crowden Clough, and not the Grinasbrook, since our actual course had long been naught but a fitful series of deviations and uncertain efforts to correct them.

Just as we emerged on the open fell-side we started a big white hare. Then we slid down a smooth shoot to the brook, and crossed to the opposite side of the valley. At each step we grew more confident of our locality, for the mist thinned after sunset, and over the white steeps and hollows the afterglow flung magical tints, revealing well-known objects whilst arraying them in somewhat of visionary glamour. High above, on the crest of Kinder, Grindsbrook Knoll stood out clear, a shapely mass of immaculate snow, catching the soft gleam that the misty sky refracted. In front of us and deep below, Edale lay obscure, the village lights quenched in a volume of blackness that seemed to be the base of a dark wall of cumulus rising to the sky and, as it were, fencing off the wild upper region of snow and ice from the milder dales. We kept well above the brook till, reaching the end of the shoulder, we had before us a smooth and open expanse of snow, down which we raced, and ten minutes later found ourselves at the inn, not very much behind the stipulated time. The eight miles had taken us seven hours, and we should have been hard put to it had we been spurred by a sterner sense of punctuality.

IX.

SCRAMBLING ON DERBYSHIRE CRAGS.

SOME apology might perhaps be needed for a series of chapters on climbs that hardly ever exceed a hundred feet in height, however excellent they might be as compact illustrations of climbing technique, were they not situated in the neighbourhood of some of the most attractive scenery in England, and right at the gates of several big towns. For most of us it is still a day's march to the hills of Cambria and of Cumbria—long may it remain so—and many a scrambler would doubtless be glad to hear of a playground where the casual holiday could be passed in the enjoyment of his favourite sport. Not long ago a handful of climbers woke up to the fact that Derbyshire contains a miniature mountain - system, amid which many capital little scrambles are to be found, nearly all within reach of even a half-day's excursion from Manchester, Sheffield, Derby, and Nottingham. There are, it is true, no laurels to be won upon the edges and monoliths of Peakland, and there is little scope for sensational exploits and hairbreadth escapes; the man who happens to tumble off a big boulder may hurt himself, but he will not have the gratification of falling through a thousand feet or so of magnificent scenery. But for such climbers as can appreciate the late Owen Glynne Jones's advice about five-foot mantelpieces, whose highest ambition is to graduate on some fancy climb in

Snowdonia or the Lake mountains, these minor heights afford many interesting and instructive lessons. We have read how the valiant Tartarin was wont to prepare for great deeds on Mont Blanc by balancing along the rim of his garden aquarium; and an esteemed friend of mine keeps his muscular mechanism in order by ascending the outside of an iron staircase on his fingers, and, after a short " stomach traverse," crossing in a sitting posture the tie-bars of the lofty roof beneath which he is doomed to spend the intervals between his holidays. But after all there is nothing like rock; and a few odd crags within handy distance of a town are worth all the banister-traverses, cast-iron *arètes*, and difficult chimney-pieces in the shire.

Most of the rock exposed in Derbyshire is either millstone grit or limestone, and the merits of gritstone are well known equally to millers and to climbers. It is solid and firm as the soundest granite, and inferior only to the gabbro of Skye as an instrument of torture, if you happen to get your hand between the rope and the rock. The characteristic feature of the grit is the abrupt escarpment called an " Edge," which fortifies many of the hill-tops. These edges abound in scrambles of various lengths; but not less useful are the isolated boulders which lie about the moors, like the Eagle Stone on Baslow Edge or the Cork and Andle Stones on Stanton Moor. The last-mentioned has a very difficult problem on the corner to the left of the public gangway. Certain of the more eminent among these gritstone notabilities will be described fully in the ensuing pages. As to the others, few perhaps are worth making a special journey to see; yet, if in the course of a day's ramble we come across two or three, they may give us excellent wayside diversion. One of the most whimsical of these insulated rocks lies on

Derwent Moor, in the middle of a walk that every lover of Derbyshire ought to be acquainted with, from Cut-throat Bridge on the Ladybower, across the gloomy solitudes of Derwent Edge, down into the lone heathery depths threaded by the Abbey Brook, a sanctuary in the wilds whose grave and sombre beauty attracts few pilgrims; and on again over Howden Moor to Slippery Stones, where the track for Langsett and Penistone strikes across the high moors between Derbyshire and Yorkshire. The whole of this region is an utter solitude in summer, in winter it is a savage wilderness. While I write these lines, the papers contain accounts of the inquest on a hapless navvy, who succumbed to the storm while fighting his way across the moor one day last winter—the body actually lay in the open until mid-summer, undiscovered by tourists, gamekeepers, or the numerous search-parties that were sent out. A strange array of stony sentinels are drawn up in rank along the edge from Hurking Stones to Back Tor; there are the Cakes of Bread and the Saltcellar, with many a curious monolith that has no official title in the heraldry of the Ordnance Survey. But the queerest of all to look at is the extraordinary cluster of immense round discs, piled above one another and apparently welded together, which is nicknamed the " Wheel Stones.'' After a few indifferent scrambles on the neighbouring tors, you will find some very tolerable ones here. The piles of discs form a group of towers, close enough together to let you work up between with back and knee, if you fail to clamber over the projecting rims. In fact, the mountaineering gymnast can exhaust his devices for twisting his body into uncomfortable shapes, in finding a way to get atop of the Wheel Stones. And the same can be said of many other lonely piles. The surface of the rock is exceedingly gritty, painfully gritty, a quality that may be held to detract somewhat from its utility as a practising ground for the novice, since he may learn to think little of feats that would be perilous on rocks of finer grain. To come across the moors on a misty day, and see these weird shapes suddenly become concrete amid the universal blankness, like some grotesque sort of ghost, is quite a sensation. It is a standing puzzle to imagine how they got left there, stranded amidst the naked levels, whilst all the contiguous rocks were planed and scoured away; they are intrinsically far more wonderful than the perched blocks and other *débris* transported by the glaciers of the ice age.

From Derwent Edge the escarpments of the grit extend due south, with several breaks and overlaps, right away to Darley Dale. Anyone who would fain vary the monotony of a walk along their crests with a scramble here and a scramble there, may get any amount of such diversion on these solitary blocks and on the cliffs of the edges. Although the Derbyshire climbs are never anything more than practice scrambles, they are in themselves very entertaining, and, like climbs of more impressive height, are found amidst fine landscapes and at the end of inspiring walks. For their purpose they are of first-class quality, and a man might serve an apprenticeship here in his " off time " which would qualify him to undertake some of the most scientific rock-work in the neighbourhood of Wastdale Head and Sligachan.

At the special request of my publisher, I have attempted to draw up a list of the best-known scrambles in the High Peak and the neighbourhood, graduated according to their relative difficulty. When I say difficult, I mean the word to connote also the adjective dangerous, in order to deter beginners from attempting those climbs that stand high in the list, unless with adequate precautions. I am only in part responsible for the arrangement of the list. It is easy enough to draw up a scale of moderate and difficult to suit one's own capabilities; it is quite another thing to avoid the personal equation, and find standards that will apply to everybody. To do that, in fact, would be utterly impossible; so I have adopted the next best plan, namely, to consult a number of friends who are well acquainted with the climbs in question, and to arrange the list as nearly as I was able in accordance with the opinions they kindly offered.

I have not included the Wharncliffe climbs or those on the Roaches. Those at the former place are very numerous, and much about the same standard of difficulty—that is, I should label the majority as " moderate," and a few as " difficult," few as " easy "; while the Staffordshire climbs are hardly well known enough even to local scramblers, and, besides that, have not yet acquired recognised names. For these reasons I thought well to omit them for the present.

EASY.

Queen's Parlour Chimney (page 93).

Weasel Pinnacle (page 103).

Alport Stone— easy way (page 88).

Fat Man's Chimney, Black Rocks (page 93).

Weston's Chimney—outside edge (page 98).

Stonnis Pinnacle, Black Rocks (page 95).

Twopenny Tube, Kinder Scout (page 115).

MODERATE.

South Gully, Black Rocks (page 93).

Downfall Corner (page 114).

Descent Perilous, Breedon (page 135).

Dolomite Steeple, Harborough Rocks (page 140).

Sgurr-na-Breedon (page 134).

Pine Tree Gully, Black Rocks (page 94).

Sand Gully, Black Rocks (page 93).

Owl Gully, Cratcliff (page 98).

East Arête, Breedon (page 136).

East Climb, Breedon (page 136).

Harborough Pinnacle (page 139).

Crazy Pinnacle, Grindleford (page 52).

Hermitage Chimney, Cratcliff (page 99).

Nether Tor, Kinder Scout (page 20).

Hemlock Stone (page 144).

Face Climb, Brassington Rocks (pages 137 and 142).

Crack and two Chimneys, Brassington Rocks (pages 136 and 142).

Long Climb, Brassington Rocks (pages 136 and 141).

North Climb, Cratcliff (page 99).

Queen's Parlour Gully (page 95).

North Crack, Robin Hood's Stride (page 105).

Fairbrook Naze Crack (page 118).

DIFFICULT.

The Nose, Breedon (page 135).

Dargai Crack, Cave Dale (page 132).

Short Climb, Inaccessible Pinnacle (page 101).

Long Climb, Inaccessible Pinnacle (page 102).

Alport Stone, Shoulder Climb (page 89).

Hemlock Stone—variations (page 145).

Harborough Chimney (page 139).

Twopenny Tube—outside route (page 115).

Weasel Pinnacle—long climb (page 104).

Stonnis Crack, Black Rocks (page 95).

X.

THE ALPORT STONE.

A S a good example of the sort of climbing offered by these isolated masses of grit, take the Alport Stone, which stands out a solitary column on the brow of a hill overlooking Wirksworth, a township not unknown to admirers of George Eliot. Here we are on the southern verge of the heather country; the great quarried precipice over yonder marks the end of the limestone tablelands that stretch drearily away to Dovedale; whilst across the spacious valley of the Ecclesbourne we look on a country-side whose beauty is quite different from that of the Peak—a tranquil beauty of hills and meadowy vales, rich woods and coverts—the naked rocks and moorlands have ended.

Our obelisk stands at the entrance to a quarry, and appears to have got its present shape partly by artificial means; yet it looks extremely life-like, and geologists will find a good sample of false bedding at the base. I had heard a most harrowing account of the sensational capabilities of the Alport Stone, before making its acquaintance; and the contemptuous regard with which it receives persons who come without an introduction has been known to scare away even an experienced member of the Alpine Club. But this reserve vanishes as soon as you know the proper way to approach the stony old patriarch. On one side, a sloping ledge leads to a perpendicular corner in which a series of notches has been weathered, and subsequently deepened by the

Photo by   *G.A. Fowkes, Derby.*

THE ALPORT STONE – EASY WAY.

THE ALPORT STONE – SHOULDER CLIMB.

ironclad toes of climbers, forming an easy ladder up
to a deep horizontal cleft that goes right through the
stone. This cleft affords hand-hold, while the knees
rest on a slender ledge, until the right hand reaches up
to an indentation on the top; and in a moment or two
the only difficult step is passed, and the climb finished.
This is the easy ascent or " Turnpike "; but the holds
are not so easy to find with the feet, and it is such a
ticklish manœuvre getting round the corner, that you
will be wise to put the rope on for the descent, unless
you are familiar with every inch of the climb. A more
expeditious way to descend is to fix the rope round a
corner at the top, and let one's self down by it on the
farther side. If half a gale is blowing—and Alport
Hill is a windy place—it is difficult to humour the rope
over this corner; as last man on top, I have often found
myself in a queer position. However, the Stone is
scarcely 40ft. high on the tallest side, so the odds are
not very fearful. I believe several scramblers have
tumbled off it with impunity.

Since the climb up the boss and shoulder at the angle
farthest from the "Turnpike" was found practicable, the
arête climb has gone out of vogue, except as a way for
invalids and ladies. The new one is decidedly stiff.
There is first of all a tussle to get atop of the boss,
which overhangs and pushes one out, and it is, moreover, much too small to accommodate a pair of climbing
boots conveniently. Every precaution will, of course,
be taken by the punctilious scrambler to avoid making
use, as finger-holds, of the initials, names, and flourishes
that have been incised on the rock by that part of
mankind which never climbs without leaving its mark.
Should you inadvertently lay hands on one of these or
use it as a toe-scraper, it is incumbent on you to descend
and make a fresh start. From the boss, or from a

half-inch ledge just above it, a finger or two can get hold of a bit of roughness high on the right, while the left foot goes on a journey of exploration round the corner, and finds a shallow depression that helps to steady the body while we swarm up, by an exhausting effort, to a narrow ledge with a bad slope outwards. For a few breathless seconds, the whole of our weight depends on certain shallow wrinkles for the finger tips, and on friction; then, by an indescribable movement, the ledge is surmounted, and the top is now within easy reach. After an hour's exercise of this kind, one is astonished to feel aches in sundry muscles as to whose existence in the human frame we usually pin our faith blindly to the anatomical chart.

The Alport Stone was the first rock I ever attempted to climb according to scientific rules and methods, and I have felt towards it ever since a peculiar affection, which the grand old crag has repaid by never treating me to any of the defeats and tumbles that less favoured scramblers have met with. An experienced climber used to tell us that the man who could ascend the Stone by the difficult way was equal to most of the favourite scrambles in Cumberland and Wales. We were sceptical then, for we felt an awful respect for the famous climbs we had heard so much about, but not yet made acquaintance with. Nevertheless, it was a true saying. The hardest British climb contains nothing appreciably harder than this shoulder climb, the Crack at the Black Rocks, the Boulder climb at Robin Hood Stride, and one or two other things the neighbourhood can boast. The great climbs are simply more extensive. And in calculating one's ability to do a lengthy rock-climb, the question of endurance is not so much to be reckoned with as may be imagined. I allude merely to physical endurance. In rock-climbing with a party, one is resting as often as one is at work; plodding up an easy mountain-side is enormously more fatiguing. The longest climb of extreme and sustained severity that I am practically acquainted with, the Crowberry Ridge on Buchaille Etive, close to Glencoe, is not long enough to tire the body, though the continual strain of new problems and new dangers on the leader's mind must be acute. In fact, the practical difference between our exceedingly hard little climbs and a big one in the mountains is a psychological difference; and, unfortunately, the training adapted thereto is scarcely to be enjoyed in Derbyshire, where you can get only hints as to the right management of the rope, and the art of feeling at ease on a dangerous face. If, however, you compare what may be called the ornamental climbs of Wastdale and other places, the Pinnacle, the Needle, and the shorter climbs on the Pillar, I think the Alport Stone can hold its own very well.

XI.

THE BLACK ROCKS, NEAR MATLOCK.

> " Here in wild pomp, magnificently bleak,
> Stupendous Matlock towers amid the Peak;
> Here rocks on rocks, on forests forests rise,
> Spurn the low earth, and mingle with the skies.
> Great Nature, slumbering by fair Derwent's stream,
> Conceived these giant mountains in a dream."

A CLIMBER who happened to read these egregious lines of the poet Montgomery, often quoted, and that approvingly, by local writers of guide-books, might get it into his head that Matlock is a promising place for a week-end at Easter; and the idea would be confirmed if he lighted on the description of the same place by a still more grandiose bard, who tells us that—

> " Mountains lower
> Abrupt: and rocks, rent, rugged, frowning, throw
> Their morning shadows o'er the stream below.
> Stern giants !" etc., etc.

Rather than be accused of luring my fellow-scramblers hither on false pretences, I will at once admit that there are no mountains at Matlock; our bards were perhaps, by a poetical or a geological licence, alluding to the far-distant past. And the only climbs I can offer as a substitute, to any one so basely disappointed, are, like the poetry, of a decidedly minor order. Yet they are good climbs in their way, and their merits have been endorsed by the approval of several renowned climbers. In Matlock itself there are practically no climbs, the limestone scrambles being very inferior; but within sight of both Matlock and Cromford, on a conspicuous

Photo by   G.A. Fowkes, Derby.
STONNIS CRACK, BLACK ROCKS, CROMFORD.

Photo by

BLACK ROCKS, CROMFORD.

G.A. Foukes, Derby.

hill-top, we meet our accommodating old friend, the millstone grit, on the Black Rocks. This picturesque group of broken cliffs and rocky needles epitomises all the varieties of gritstone climbs in small compass. There is a rectangular cleft, 40ft. high and 30ft. deep, which can give some first-rate back-and-knee work; but every climber who is not abnormally thin is advised to take off his coat, if he venture further in than the outside edge of the chimney. I have seen a member of the Alpine Club totally unable to ascend a shorter but wider cleft (South Gully) that is a harder test of strength and skill, owing to the absence of all holds but so-called friction holds. A still more extraordinary chimney, at the farther end of the cliff, takes the climber on a darksome journey into the entrails of the rock, and he wriggles up into a small cave known as the " Queen's Parlour," out of which he makes his way by the window on to a fine balcony, near the top of the crags, with a view which might figure handsomely among the marketable attractions of the Parlour, were it ever to let.

But the best scrambling is to be had on the two steepest gullies. One of them, which consists of three steep pitches, bears the name of the Sand Gully. The first man who climbed it thought he had performed a philanthropic work, by sweeping down hundredweights of coarse sand, and nearly blinding his companion; but Nature's resources are inexhaustible, and every winter she refills the crevices and hand-holds, and smothers the first party who come up in spring. Of the three pitches, the middle one is the most severe. A steep wall, 12ft. high, fills the gully just here, quite smooth, but for one slight depression hardly worth calling a ledge, which forms a resting-place for a knee half-way up. Near this there is a curious little slit, easily overlooked, which may be utilised cunningly to steady oneself in descending without a rope. With a good long reach, you may get athwart the gully, with one foot against the side, whilst your hands cautiously approach a crevice on the top corner. Or you may get a knee on the depression already mentioned, and, straightening yourself gradually, use the smooth top of the wall as a hold for the forearms; this is safe and satisfactory, but requires skill and care. Above the pitch the gully is straitened by the intrusion of a vertical block. The best way to finish is to turn one's back to the gully, and propel one's self up with feet and hands on the two side walls. It is advisable to use the rope always in this short climb; a great many tumbles have occurred on the middle pitch. Pine Tree Gully is longer, but not quite so good. (The pine-root half-way up and the trunk near the top, which gave it the name, have for some time been dislodged.) At the bottom there is a very awkward chimney, which is sometimes avoided by slim people, and a sort of needle's eye, under a jammed stone, threaded instead. But the chimney is well worth doing, and, taken regularly, would be an efficacious cure for obesity. I have seen a man struggle at it, without avail, so long and so desperately that he got an attack of that dolorous ailment, Climber's Chest, characterised chiefly by acute aches in the region of the breast bone; it lasted nearly a week. The rest of the gully can be climbed in various ways. Perhaps the finest method for those who can stand the strain, is to back up, walking on the right wall with the back to the left wall; and the next best is to sit in the gully, and lever one's self up with the feet against the sides.

A little to the right of this climb, I got into an awkward scrape at my first visit to the Black Rocks, with no rope and no nails in my boots. At an exposed spot one of my boots got jammed in a crevice, and I was totally unable to pull it out. A friend was obliged ultimately to climb to the rescue, and lever it out with a walking stick. Such little incidents illustrate the prudence of not attempting even easy scrambling without a companion. There are many other scrambles and problems that may fill up the measure of a long afternoon's enjoyment; a queer little gully outside the Queen's Parlour; a gothic pinnacle, not far away, on which some Philistine has chopped hand-holds that are quite unnecessary; and a second pinnacle, not quite so handsome, that marks the beginning of an unsafe and exciting scramble to the top of the cliff.

But the best of these—and, indeed, the stiffest thing here—is the Crack, a fissure, some 25ft. long, that splits the smooth face near the Sand Gully. This is a problem climb in the simplest form. It has no extraneous attractions, none but the danger of a nasty fall, an attraction that has been carefully eliminated hitherto by consistent use of the rope; it leads nowhither, and is of no account except as an admirable test of finger-work and the art of balancing. At the bottom, a foot-hold about shoulder-high is easily reached by pulling up with the hands; then, inserting the left foot into the widest part of the crack, the climber ascends the first few feet at an angle of 80°. When the edges of the cleft become too much rounded to be used for gripping, the necessary hand-hold may be had by thrusting one's hands into the rift as far as they will go—if your skin is proof against gritstone. Half-way up a flake of rock divides the crack for several feet. There the proper move is to stretch up with the right hand and insert one stout finger, or even two of moderate size, into a little hole that seems to have been made for the purpose. It is the only genuine hold till you are close to the top. This steadies the body for a few palpitating moments; and now, pushing bravely up, you thrust your left into the overhanging part of the crack, and the horizontal traverse is within reach. Now comes the tug-of-war. You are probably done up, or nearly so, unless you have wasted no time in bungling and puffing; but, before you can take breath, there is a hand-traverse of several feet to be tackled, along a flattish edge with no definite grip, so that you support yourself merely on the arms while the legs dangle. This is arduous, but you will do it after a few tries; but when, with such inadequate support, you have to shift your body and legs up sideways to the ledge, you will find the moral influence of the rope a real comfort. Once arrived on the ledge, you may struggle up a vertical joint to the grass plot above, or get astride of a smooth ridge that ascends to the same plot at an angle of 30°. Though I have frequently ascended the Crack on a slack rope, I should say that to attempt it without the rope at all is a very dangerous and a perfectly useless feat.

Shun the Black Rocks at holiday times. Everything in the fair prospect laid out before you has been inventoried and described in a dozen guide-books, and is then on view. This is a nice, secluded spot for a picnic; but it is embarrassing for both parties when a climber gets to the top of a gully and suddenly finds himself figuring at one of these quiet social functions as an object of strange and absorbing interest. At ordinary times, however, there is no quieter or less hackneyed spot, and the climber looks down on the dale and woody heights of Matlock, the splintered cliffs, and the river, from his ledge high above the tree-tops, perfectly safe from inquisitive tourists.

XII.

CRATCLIFF TOR.

FROM the Black Rocks, a romantic walk by way
of the Via Gellia and Winster can be taken to
Robin Hood's Stride. The vents of two volcanoes
are passed near Grange Mills, both of them now extinct,
unfortunately for climbers, who would welcome the
upheaval of a good snow-peak in the neighbourhood.
A short time ago it was seriously reported that an
eruption had occurred at Ambergate; the rumour probably had some connection with the ironworks in the
vicinity. The Stride can also be reached by a pretty
ramble from Darley Dale Station over the ridge of
Cowley, which surveys two dales, and across Stanton
Moor, which commands views of the Derwent and the
Wye, with a glimpse of the wooded brink of Lathkill
Dale. Haddon Hall, seen from the Andle Stone—or,
the Twopenny Loaf, as the yokels call it—has the air
of a baronial mansion still in its prime, and transports
the spectator back in memory to the days when it held
sway over the broad tracts of hill and vale outstretched
around him. As we run down the hill to Birchover,
the Stride comes into view with striking effect, high on
the crest of a hill. The rocky knoll forming the summit
of the hill is shaped like a high-pitched roof, with the two
rock-towers called the Stride perched like Elizabethan
chimneys on its gable-ends. Between us and this quaint
pile rise the cliffs of Cratcliff Tor, weather-worn and
rifted into fantastic masses that seem ever on the point

G

of overwhelming the lovely woods beneath. Look where you will, rocky tors are islanded by woods, where oak and Spanish chestnut make a brave show of colour in autumn and spring.

A broad gap sunders the two main cliffs of Cratcliff Tor. It is filled with a chaotic jumble of fallen blocks, that look as if the hill had been shaken by earthquake; and in and out among the masses of gritstone a labyrinth of chimneys and gullies winds about, including one, at least, which is a good place for back-and-knee work. It goes up aslant, whilst another chimney, named after an explorer of the Japanese Alps, is vertical. It is a place where fat men must needs take off their jackets. Any one who likes, can turn this short problem into a longer climb, by ascending an irregular and rather dirty chimney from the cliff's base some 60ft. below.

The grandest feature on the front of the Tor is the vertical gash a little way to the north, cutting straight from top to bottom. The walls of this gully are over 100ft. high, the rock-climb is a good 80ft., and it is decidedly the most showy thing in the neighbourhood. A 12ft. wall barricades the entrance to the gully; and when this has been surmounted by means of a little shelf half-way up, a nasty plot of loose soil, held together with blackberry brambles, has to be crossed, and requires caution. You then enter the extreme corner of the cleft, and the rest of the ascent is straightforward chimney work, with no superabundant supply of holds, till the jammed block is reached. On making my first ascent, I had wriggled up the vertical section till I found myself under this projecting block, which completely cut off my view of the upper part. The top of the gully overhangs four or five feet; it is highly sensational though safe to a steady head, as I found out afterwards. What with the apprehension of difficulties hid by the

WESTON'S CHIMNEY, CRATCLIFF TOR.
(A Derbyshire Memory of Owen Glynne Jones).

Photo by   *G.A. Fowkes, Derby.*

THE OWL GULLY, CRATCLIFF TOR.

Photo by   G.A. Fowkes, Derby.

NORTH CLIMB, CRATCLIFF TOR.

Photo by   G.A. Fowkes, Derby.

HAND TRAVERSE ON ROW TOR.

stone, and a keen sense that a return would be worse than the ascent had been, I began to repent not having made a previous survey on the rope. Nobody was to be seen or heard, the rest of the party being busy in the central gully; but, after I had hung in an awkward position for some time, succour came, and the rope was let down from the platform overhead. It was well that the friendly hemp was at hand, for just as my head came over the jammed stone, there was a fierce flapping of wings and out rushed a large owl into my face, nearly startling me off my perch. To finish the gully it was necessary to go right through the nest, for the cavernous hole formed by the jammed stone had clearly been his residence from of old, and was a silent witness that the gully had not been invaded for the last few years at least. A few weeks ago I found the Owl's Nest and every nook and cranny swarming with young jackdaws, plump and vociferous, but too weak on their legs to stand. The place is inaccessible to schoolboys, or they would soon have been made into a pie. To surmount the slabs that roof it in, one must come out, bestride the chasm, and pull one's self over to the right wall. The full-length view of the Owl Gully thus disclosed between one's legs is very fine; the side walls are as clean cut as if one of those American quarrying engines had shaped them, and the non-climbing friends who have come out to laugh at us are right underneath, startled into interest in spite of themselves.

Among various other climbs that need not be particularised on this gnarled and shattered precipice, there is a good 30ft. crack in an angle only a few steps from the Owl Gully. It belongs to the *facilis descensus* variety, and, after swarming down it, you will be astonished at the stubborn resistance it offers to a re-ascent. The Hermitage Chimney has only one defect, it is too short. Many feet beneath it, screened by an ancient yew, is the Anchorite's Cell, with the weathered crucifix still conspicuous on the wall. From our airy perch above it we peer into mysterious depths of foliage, and the rocks and bracken on the hillside are visible only in patches. The hermit must surely have had an eye for romantic scenery. What would he have thought, I wonder, of the barbarous iron railing that has of late been fixed across the entrance to his asylum? Apparently there has always been a mysterious sanctity about Cratcliff Tor and its immediate environs. The Druids had a "connection" there, as the stone circle behind the summit proves (the neighbouring tavern is still called "The Druid," as if to commemorate the week-day profession of the local incumbent); then came the Christian anchorite; and now, centuries later, the Methodists hold a conventicle or camp-meeting there yearly. And all this time the crags have been lying fallow, waiting for some one to come and climb them.

I have omitted to mention a neat little scramble that is visible from Cratcliff on the end of Row Tor, the curious pile of heaped-up rocks, covered with trees, at whose farther end is the Druid Inn. This climb is worth doing on the way hither. Once a climber arrived by this route, apparently from nowhere, right in the midst of an *al fresco* tea-party, who were quietly sitting on the edge of the cliff in a spot that old tacticians would certainly have deemed impregnable. The incident was startling to both sides. This scramble involves an excellent little hand-traverse.

XIII.

ROBIN HOOD'S STRIDE.

O N the Stride, which is only a bow-shot away
from Cratcliff Tor, there are a number of nondescript scrambles, ranging from the easy to
the supremely difficult, though none are long enough
to tax anyone's endurance. The finest of the twin
summits nicknamed Robin Hood's Stride has been
compared by a great authority on rock-climbing, the
ill-fated Owen Glynne Jones, with some of the stiffest
short climbs in the Alps; and recently another accomplished climber pronounced it a match for the well-known
Napes Needle in Cumberland. Though still called the
" Inaccessible," to distinguish it from its brother
pinnacle, whose capture is an affair of much less
moment, it has now for many years been subject to
erosion by hobnailed boots. It has three faces of
respectable height; but on the fourth, the floor of
boulders that tops the roof-shaped knoll is only 10ft.
below the summit of the pinnacle; yet the upper edge
overhangs so much, and there is such a drop on each
side, that it would be hard to find a climb at once
so short and so severe. The first step is to get a knee
on a sloping buttress to the left, the second to wedge
the fingers into a vertical crack, and so lever one's self
to a posture nearly erect under the overhanging part.
Then a questionable grip is felt for over the edge, while
the left boot gets a nail-hold on a tiny notch; and now
you heave yourself slowly and painfully over the top

edge. Whether this feat is performed with facility and grace, depends a great deal on whether you are on good terms with the inner man. If the climber be puffed and flabby, the tussle will needs be prolonged and unseemly before he is safely over the parapet. A record office was opened at the summit of this important peak in the shape of a tin box for visiting cards; before, however, many distinguished names were collected, the box was rifled by " jackdaws."

The cliff on the opposite side of the same pinnacle might be likened to a cheap edition of one face of the Pillar Rock; for it has a chimney, with a Pendlebury traverse, an *arête*, and a notch climb above it. Please do not smile because the whole crag would make but a modest church steeple; you will find that the same scale applies to the ledges and the finger-holds, which is an important compensation. At the bottom a ponderous boulder leans against the rock, as if to protect it from assault. So utterly impossible does the boulder look that neither we nor anybody else seem to have thought of attempting an ascent just here, until we were nettled by the chaff of a critic who had always met our reports of new climbs with the retort, " Oh, but you haven't done the ' Inaccessible ' yet right from the bottom ! " And so we made a desperate attempt, and after one or two tries I found myself, much to my surprise, on top of the obstacle. Were the rock anything else than millstone grit the climb would probably remain unaccomplished still; but one can do anything on the grit, so long as one does not mind the scars and smarts inflicted by its sharp granular surface and the ruinous friction on one's clothes. With a half-leap the climber seizes the leaf of rock presented at one corner. Holds there are none; he hangs on by gripping the attenuated corner in an occult manner

Photo by   *G.A. Fowkes, Derby.*

THE INACCESSIBLE PINNACLE – ROBIN HOOD'S STRIDE.

Photo by   *Bird and Co., Stamford.*

ROBIN HOOD'S STRIDE – 'THE BOULDER'.

Photo by   *G.A. Fowkes, Derby.*

WEASEL PINNACLE – ROBIN HOOD'S STRIDE.

with knees and elbows, while he wriggles straight up, inch by inch, until, just as his wind is exhausted, a hand can be got over into a saucer on top. This is not bad as a muscular feat, but the choicest bit is near the finish, where he walks sideways for several yards along a horizontal crack for the toes, his hands pressed against " friction holds," while nothing but a delicate sense of gravity saves him from tumbling backwards down the crags. Once get a leg into the twisted crevice at the far corner, and a little more energy takes you to the top. The upper part of the turret is sculptured by storm and frost into all fantastic shapes; but the filigree work on the cornice should not be trusted too freely for holds; a projection that looked quite solid has before now come off in my hand like a piece of cake. There is a handsome belaying-pin amongst the other natural furniture on the top, and much confidence can be instilled into a nervous person coming up by pretending to give the rope a twist round it.

The Weasel Pinnacle, separated from this by the giant stride of athletic Robin Hood—a matter of twenty paces—offers no such opportunities for refined art as this; yet it boasts of three ways up, two of them far from obvious, while the frontal climb is a first-rate test for the man—

" Derbyshire born and Derbyshire bred,
Strong in the arm, weak in the head ;"

though weakness in the head is not a positive advantage even on these miniature summits. Only the last time I was there the accuracy of the test was verified when a Yorkshireman, weak in the arms, but evidently strong otherwise, came tumbling backwards ere I could save him a hard bump on the rocky pavement. The face of this turret is deeply grooved with flutings, much deeper than those of a Doric column, and the way to ascend it is to push the arms into these grooves and wriggle up by main force. There is not enough of it to make the struggle interesting, but the long face on the opposite side is so continuously difficult that I for one should decline to attempt it without the rope, though I have done it repeatedly on a slack one. Between these scrambles, on a third face which appears destitute of holds, is another little climb that is a puzzle to the uninitiated and a trial to the best man's nerve.*

Even on our minor summits on the Derbyshire hills, people sometimes get scared. Once on ascending the Inaccessible by way of the boulder, we discovered 35ft. of Alpine rope tightly but nervously attached to a projection, with the end hanging over and cut. Who were the party of terrified cragsmen, so hopeless of getting down, that they sacrificed the " moral support " so barefacedly ? They never called again for their rope. The fine boulder north of the Stride has three or four problems on it, for balance and finger-work, and is quite as good as the well-known Muscle Boulder at the top of Stye Head Pass.

The Stride and Cratcliff Tor together make just the right sort of place for the initiation of candidates to scansorial honours. As I have shown, difficult climbs are not scarce there; and, on the other hand, there are abundant scrambles exactly suited for beginners. There is an enormous boulder not far below the Weasel Pinnacle, between it and the vale, which I should recommend a novice to seek out. It can be recognised by the cave underneath it, which is floored with dry sand and would make an excellent spot for a bivouac. It marks the beginning of an irregular series of pitches and traverses that lead across the chaos of weathered

---

* The one tiny rock flake that made this little climb feasible has unfortunately broken away recently.

blocks to the Weasel Pinnacle itself, which crowns the wild edifice fitly. Anyone who has a fancy for a short climb that is as difficult as this is easy, will find a steep crack on the north side of the tor, facing the great boulder that has so many problems on it. How to arrive on the ledge surmounting a square corner is the initial puzzle; then the hard work begins. The crack goes straight up a slanting cliff. It has a facile look about it; but, though the slope is moderate, there are no holds. From the bottom to the top it is simply a tug-of-war with gravity; and as your only ally is friction, you will leave the thing respectfully alone if you have any regard for your clothes.

XIV.

ON WHARNCLIFFE CRAGS, NEAR SHEFFIELD.

TO tell an enthusiastic rock-climber that there are plenty of good " chimneys " at Sheffield would doubtless be resented as a criminal attempt at a joke. " Chimneys " there are, however, and of the right sort, just outside the steel city; and Sheffield may reasonably esteem itself better off than any other large town in England as a residence for mountaineers. Edinburgh alone, with the crags of Arthur's Seat hanging over its very streets, can be compared with it. When a Sheffield friend told me this, and invited me to bring a party for an afternoon's scrambling on Wharncliffe Crags, I was surprised and a little incredulous, though well aware that he was not the man to be satisfied with anything of inferior quality. Our visit proved the truth of his boast. Wharncliffe is almost a suburb of Sheffield. Yet, were one to reckon up the problems, great and small, to be met with on this long mile of crag, they would easily number two score. To be sure, they are little climbs, varying from 20ft. to 60ft. in height; but what does it matter ? Climbing is a sport as well as a branch of travel; and when mountaineering is not to be had, an ardent climber may well be satisfied with the athletics of the game, particularly if he can reach his playground in half an hour.

Photo by   H. Lygo.

AN AWKWARD FISSURE.

Photo by

LONG JOHN'S STRIDE.

H. Eggleston.

Strolling up through woods and bushy glades, more like a forest than a park (a queer place to lose one's self in at night, as I know by painful experience), we emerge on a scarped hill-crest just like a Derbyshire edge. Miles of woodland stretch away behind; below the rocky bulwark deep woods slope to the bottom of the valley. We recognise our familiar and trusted friend, the millstone grit, and think we know what awaits us. But our Sheffield friends can teach us something yet, for here they have reduced climbing to a systematic art, and can show a variety of problems graduated for the novice or the expert, and compassed about with as many rules and prohibitions as those of the smartest gymnasium.

With scant consideration for our feelings, the Sheffielders introduce us at once to what they describe as a difficult rock-face. It looks so ugly that we decline to try it without a rope from the top. The rope is provided, and for half an hour we each in turn execute a series of acrobatic ascents and tumbles, but get up it we cannot. Then we are told, with what looks like a sarcasm, that the climb has not yet been finished, but has been reserved for our special entertainment. To enumerate the different species of cracks, chimneys, buttresses, hand-traverses, strides, and chockstones, over which we are now escorted, would be tiresome. At one spot a little cove, surrounded by towers of gritstone, gives immediate access to seven or eight distinct climbs, mostly difficult. The first chimney is nearly all chockstone, one specimen sticking out above another in a way that necessitates some remarkable posturing. One of the most characteristic performances at this spot hardly comes under the head of rock-climbing at all. This is the Wharncliffe method of crossing fissures and gaps. Stand bolt upright on the edge of a rock tower, facing another rock tower that is sundered from yours by a chasm 50ft. deep. Throw your arms straight up, then bend forward stiffly till the hands touch the opposite wall and your body bridges the gap. Bringing one foot forward to steady yourself, you drop your body across and rest on the edge of the tower by the forearms, then lift yourself into safety by a movement of the wrists. If this is not sufficient test for nerves and sinews, then step this way and look at the "Monkey Jump." It is not a wide jump, only 5ft., from a shelf of rock to another shelf three feet lower. But the latter is overhung by a mass of rock that compels one to twist slightly in mid-air so as to arrive in a stooping position. The muscular feat is trifling, the nerve test tremendous. I have a photograph of a man in the act of leaping, but it is blurred, and only good enough to verify my description. Hard by is another innocent-looking problem, a corner with sloping top that has to be scaled by means of a peculiar lift with the forearms, with a tumble into a rocky gully for the forfeit.

Our Sheffield hosts are in the habit—from strictly scientific motives, of course—of eliminating the more convenient holds from any given climb, much in the way a crafty examiner leaves out the handiest logarithms; and so they can set the new-comer some particularly severe exercises. A certain face climb, for instance, was stiffened by the imaginary removal of a large boulder; and it was gratifying to the Sheffielders to see how regularly their guests dropped off on the rope as, one by one, they reached the level of this desirable stone. A good deal of diversion was created by a non-climbing visitor. Two experienced men had struggled with much display of science up a short but difficult cleft, when this gentleman, after watching them

critically, called out, " But why don't you chaps do it
this way?" and forthwith ran up the cliff after the
manner of a cat storming a garden wall, quite heedless
of the fact that he ought to have had nails in his boots.
This gentleman must be kept out of the Climbers' Club
at all hazards, for climbing will soon cease to be an art
if our pet scrambles are to be massacred in such
unceremonious fashion.

The Wharncliffe grit is exceptionally angular, and
the corners that are so handy to clutch deprive us, as
we go, of a good deal of cuticle. One man got pilloried
in the very middle of a narrow rift, which did not allow
room for him to turn round, while he clung to the sharp
edges till a rope was let down from the cliff-top. The
next chimney has a chock-stone of superior quality near
the foot. This might be evaded if we chose; but we
are sternly admonished to climb it fairly, for are we
not come out on purpose to ascend obstacles? Backing
up the chimney, whose blank walls converge at an acute
angle, we approach the top, and in a critical situation
have to perform a right-about-face, and fling our hands
against the other wall, so as to circumvent a protruding
stone that nearly blocks up the aperture.

Whenever a friendly but unrecognised rock offers
assistance to a baffled climber, the warning, " Hands
off!" bids us mind the strict rule of the game. We
tumble on the rope again and again; there is no shirking
the salutary discipline. And when at length we retire,
all battered, and hot and dusty, to refreshing ablutions
in the buckets and tubs at Wharncliffe Lodge, we rack
our brains to think of some climbs of exceptional
roughness and severity, with jagged corners and
impossible chockstones, wherewith to repay in kind the
hospitality of Sheffield.

XV.

SCRAMBLES ON KINDER SCOUT.

WHEN we left town it was a brilliant July morning and the atmosphere so strangely clear that distant objects were defined with as much sharpness and intensity as if one looked through a powerful lens. It seemed ridiculous to trouble about taking a compass; surely there was no fear to-day of getting befogged on the moors. But as soon as we left Edale and set our faces towards the steep zigzags of Jacob's Ladder we found we had made a mistake. The dale was clear and sunny, but the top of Cowburn and the edges of Kinder Scout were concealed in a bank of fog, out of which milk-white streams of vapour crept down the watercourses, and down the side of every wall like streams of water, though without the swiftness of water and without its noise.

My companion and I kept religiously to the right of way, for the friend who held our passport into the neighbouring territory of rock, bilberry, and peat moss was waiting for us somewhere higher up. On meeting him we turned forthwith towards the Scout, and, crossing the head of the clough where lie the ultimate springs of the River Noe, we directed our steps towards a clump of rocks towering like a shattered castle on the skirts of the fog. Without a moment's delay a keeper was on our track (how carefully this important frontier is guarded!), and he looked so disappointed to find we were not unlicensed trespassers that we gave him a smoke to soothe his mortification. When we came near enough to see them clearly the clump of rocks dwindled to insignificance, only affording a 12ft. scramble. We visited the summit of Kinder Low, generally supposed to be Kinder's highest point, though a less prominent part of the Scout is a few feet higher. Then we began to pick our steps carefully, for sky and landmarks were completely blotted out, and we must make a straight line across the dreary moss-hags, nor'-nor'-east, for the Downfall, as best we might. The map was of little use without a compass. We got a furlong or so out of our way, and found ourselves on the edge just where the Red Brook cuts through. This spot a few years ago vied with the Downfall's rugged gorge in grandeur of rock scenery. Read L. J. Jennings's fine description in " Rambles among the Hills " (now unfortunately out of print), and then observe this notable object-lesson in the rapidity with which the face of nature is altered. The scarps are smoothed away, the jagged boulders entombed, and the deep ravine well-nigh filled up by the movements of the peat moss and the growth of vegetation, chiefly bilberry and ling. But for the unchanged background of dale and moor some photographs I have of the once rocky clough would be unrecognisable now.

We had no further difficulty in locating the Downfall. The rope was soon out of the bag and we were looking round for the scrambles. Although the crags that hem us in at the top of the clough are fine to look at, continuous climbs are not very obvious. Nevertheless there are several scrambles of an excellent minor order, say, of 8oft. or so, that are worth hunting for; they make up in technical points for their deficiencies in extent. Is this a climb in the square corner to the north of the Downfall, where a shapeless pile of rock, one rounded projection sticking out above another, abuts against a blank wall? Two of us are inclined to pass it by, but the third declares it is worth trying. He is certainly the right one to manufacture a climb, if the article is not to be found ready made. He looks on while the two of us struggle amain to surmount the first projection without getting hopelessly jammed beneath the second. On no account will he assent to our suggestion that we should try it first with a rope from above, a practice that he usually reverses, getting up a new climb first of all by a *coup de main*, and then, if need be, studying it in detail on the rope. Above the jutting rock was a hole, and then another rock projecting still further. This latter was what made us boggle. Our leader clambered over the first projection and plunged bodily into the hole, looking like a fugitive rat with his upper quarters out of sight. He rested a few moments in this ungraceful attitude, then, holding on to nothing, he backed a few inches, and a hand and an arm came slowly out of the hole and groped about for something prehensible overhead. Then, rising to his knees, he pulled himself over the obstruction, and there was nothing remaining but an easy scramble to the cliff top. Our agonies and contortions in following, even with the rope to comfort us, were extreme.

We scrambled down the rocks of the Downfall itself to reach the foot of our next climb. The stream had shrunk to a mere driblet, although the ledges were very wet, and the cave, where we have lunched more than once when the fall was icebound, was dripping now like Roger Rain's House. Among other trifles, we had noticed a fine crack, about 8oft. high, on the massive cliff that makes such an imposing object to the north of the ravine. We plumed ourselves on a find that looked

Photo by   Richard Keene, Ltd., Derby.

THE DOWNFALL IN SUMMER.

(The Photo of the Frozen Downfall was taken from the slopes on the right.)

scarcely inferior to the famous Kern Knotts Crack at Wastdale. The bottom part is a roomy chimney, diminishing upwards. We found good holds inside; then we jammed ourselves into the narrowing cleft, first our bodies, then our legs; and as the chimney shrunk to a crack we gripped the edge of it and scraped with our toes on the outside of the cliff. All went well till the first man got within 6ft. of the top; then we saw him painfully wrestling with something, we knew not what, for the climb looked straightforward enough from below. He came back, and sent me up to try my luck. The impediment was 2ft. of smooth rock, over which it seemed absolutely impossible to climb by any fair means. One of us went round to the top with the rope, but we did not want to use that illegitimately. To make a climb of it at all we had to come down 15ft. and work our way across the sheer cliff to a beautiful little balancing problem, in a dangerous spot, a yard or two from the exit of our crack.

A nice assortment of slanting chimneys and gullies attracted us to the neighbouring recess; but time was flying, and we had an eye on a scramble at the south side. My friends, however, obligingly let me descend, with the aid of the rope, the longest and dirtiest of the lot, a fine chimney, and sooty—at all events, it was years since it had been swept, and the grit dust that lined it was black with weathered lichen and decayed peat. My appearance when I emerged was so disgraceful that I felt it would be impossible to go home before dark. This was one of the climbs that ought decidedly to be explored first of all with a rope from above, for half-way down I dropped into a nest of loose stones. When touched, a number of these jumped clean out of the gully and cleared a long stretch of hillside before they hit anything. We thought the

H

noise they made in Kinder Clough would raise the echoes all the way down to Hayfield.

Our last scramble was right in the south corner of the Downfall, first up a staircase of wet ledges that would be impassable were much water coming over, and then up a steep cleft with a jammed stone in it; altogether some 120ft. of interesting rock. And now it was time to be off homewards. We coasted along the hillocky slopes under the edge, and were successful in finding Kinder Low again in spite of the mist. Then something inexplicable happened. We ran down the knoll, as we imagined, in the direction of Edale. There was very little scope for going wrong, but we appear to have made the most of it. We came across a shooter's track, which we certainly had not noticed in the morning, but we thought it must surely lead to the public way at Jacob's Ladder. On we went downhill until the mist grew thin, and then we saw, far off in the valley—not Edale, but the roofs and chimneys of Hayfield. We had gone north instead of south; and now we must return up that weary path, which had never seemed so rough or so steep, to the top of the pass, and so over to Edale and the Nag's Head, where the kettle had been singing for tea at least half an hour ago.

Some friends discovered an excellent climb on the great mass of rocks overlooking the ravine on the south side, about a hundred yards below the Downfall, and we explored it on a much later visit. A deep irregular cleft cuts into the mass of rock, the one wall of it coming forward, square and smooth, several yards in advance of the other, which, in fact, is almost all cut away, leaving only a series of projections on that side, like tongues of rock. At the bottom the cleft is very deep, and in its extreme corner a cave gives access to a dark funnel or chimney running up inside the cliff, after the manner of the Queen's Parlour chimney at the Black Rocks. This forms an easy, but somewhat uncleanly, scramble of a hundred feet or so, and has been called, not inappropriately, the "Twopenny Tube." Our climb, which is immensely superior in sporting quality to the inside route, was up the outside edge of the cleft, in the daylight. Coming second on the rope, I clambered to a good height inside the cleft, so as to be above, or, at least, on a level with, the leader, whilst he was at grips with the obstacles of the first twenty or thirty feet, as a tumble was by no means a remote possibility. The first few lifts are easy, for the lower part of the great sheer wall, which the climber faces all the way up, is weathered into useful nicks and crevices; but the rock quickly grows smoother, and the resistance more pronounced.

Through the narrow cleft in front of me, I had glimpses of my friend working his way up; now an arm and shoulder, now a slice of his face, then all I could see were his legs and boots. The first move was to clamber up the tongues of rock, which he kept behind him; then with left arm thrust far into the cleft and the shoulder jammed not very securely, he struggled upwards, chiefly by means of friction, against the sheer wall facing him. As I found when my own turn came, this first sixty or seventy feet is a stiff trial for both muscle and nerve, the holds being so slight, and the exposure so complete. Now, all that I could see of him was a hobnailed boot, next he disappeared above me, and all we were aware of was the grating of his nails against the rock, and the chips and dirt that fell on our heads. I think our complaints of these scavenging operations only brought down a few extra shovelfuls. At length the noise ceased, and I received the summons,

" Friend, come up higher." " What sort of a place are you in ? " " Fairly precarious," he replied—an ironical phrase of his that we understood exactly. Scrambling a few feet up, over the rocky tongues, I gave him rope enough to climb into a safer position; then I spread myself over the smooth face in front, got what little support I could by wedging arm and shoulder into the fissure, and pushed strenuously on. The worst difficulty in the critical portion was, I found, the impossibility of seeing the foot-holds. There are not many; and with one's face flattened against the cliff so that one can look neither sideways nor downwards, the feet are at a disadvantage in finding these. Our leader suggested that a periscope, such as submarines use, would be a useful addition to the climber's equipment. By just dropping it over one's shoulders, one could climb down a cliff as easily as up, not to mention the advantage it would give one in such awkward situations as the present. I found our foremost man ensconced in a little cave, to approach which I had to go through a series of ungainly posturings, for the shape of the rocks was unaccommodating and the holds were quite inadequate. Nor was the ceremony of changing places with the man in possession without its difficulties, the cave-mouth being like the front passage of a jerry-built villa, not built for two people to pass. I wriggled in head first, whilst he pushed himself past by sections; then I coiled the rope, and kept an eye on him whilst he ascended to the next cave, a storey higher. Arriving there, he tightened the rope on me whilst I belayed the third man. The latter had only got up a few yards, as we knew by the scraping of boots against rock, when I felt a tremendous pull on the rope, and, simultaneously, heard the crash of rocks falling down the hillside. What had happened I could not see, for he was right underneath me, but hidden from view by the mass of the cliff projecting between us. We learned afterwards that one of the tongues or rocky projections we had both laid all our weight upon in ascending had given way beneath him. He had been saved by the rope, and the broken rock had fallen clear; yet the incident made us feel uncomfortable when we considered what might have been the result had the accident occurred whilst the leader was testing the rock, or whilst the third man was beneath it. When the latter drew nigh the middle cave, I crept out so as to give him admittance, and joined the leader up aloft, who then, in his turn, attacked the final pitch. The sporting excellences of the climb were sustained to the last. The topmost corner was a problem that each man solved in a fashion peculiar to himself; the solution offered by the leader being the most graceful, at least from my point of view immediately beneath him; for as his legs rose into the air whilst he scrambed over the edge, he looked as if he were going to stand upon his head, as a grand *finale* to his interesting contortions.

Whilst clambering down the wet rocks of the Downfall, after finishing this scramble, I saw a pretty phenomenon. I had chosen the south side as a moderately dry route, the main body of the stream coming down on the north; but just as I was hanging by the fingers on the bottom ledges, I was suddenly enveloped in a shower of spray. Then I noticed that the waterfall acted somewhat like an intermittent stream, the wind evidently holding the water back and then releasing it, so that the heaps of fallen rocks were now surrounded by a foaming mill-race, and now almost deserted by the current. In one of the lulls, I ran across the water-channel, but did not escape a drenching when the next quick burst of water came over. I rejoined my two friends, and we took our way straight across the peat moss to Fairbrook Naze.

The last time we were there, this noble mass of cliffs had struck us as an excellent field for scrambling; now, whether we were too tired to seek them out, or whether many good climbs are not to be found, we did not come across anything of note. Our flagging energies were contented with one scramble on the section of straight and comparatively unbroken cliff near the south end of the Naze. The cliff just there is divided into two storeys by a deep horizontal groove, evidently formed by the weathering away of a softer bed of rock. A perpendicular fissure ascends to this groove, whilst another chimney or fissure proceeds, at the distance of a few yards, from the groove to the cliff-top. The ascent of the first fissure presented no difficulty. My companion, who had led so ably in the last climb, followed me up, and took his station on the overhung shelf formed by the aforesaid groove, whilst I attempted the second chimney, a much more serious affair. He said afterwards that he did not like his position at all, for he could not see what I was at, on account of the rock overhanging him, and was haunted by a presentiment that I should come tumbling out of the fissure, and pull him headlong from his unprotected ledge. Straddling across a gap in the ledge I stood on, and stretching up to my full height to reach the bottom of the chimney, I got a trusty grip and pulled myself in. Once there, with back to one wall and feet against the other, I levered myself skywards by inches. At the most constricted part, the friction was tremendous, for some 30ft. of manilla rope was wound across my chest, and the rasping of this and the scraping of my hobnails against the coarse gritstone made such a hideous noise that, I suppose, my comrade underneath felt quite nervous. Grappling with some big splinters, whose character for steadiness was rather questionable, I released myself from this prolonged squeeze, and mounted over a confusion of gritstone blocks to the summit of the edge.

Another climb that is to be found on the southern cliffs of the Downfall's ravine, a little way below the " Twopenny Tube," ought to be mentioned, although I have not done it. My friends say it is first-rate, and its length, about 150ft., combined with its evident severity, entitles it to high rank among our Derbyshire scrambles, few of which exceed a hundred feet in height.

XVI.

ON THE STAFFORDSHIRE ROACHES.

THERE is nothing in Derbyshire so closely resembling a miniature range of mountains as the Roaches, the lofty gritstone ridge that dominates the borders of smoky Staffordshire, and supports a group of rocky peaks within full view of the chimney-stalks and dingy warehouses of Leek. We have here a bit of real highland scenery—cliffy hill-tops and heathery braes, with woods of pine underneath, and a solitude that is all the more delectable because we are only a few miles from a dense manufacturing population. In configuration this strip of country belongs by nature to the Peak; the gritstone whimsicalities of such spots as Robin Hood's Stride, the Black Rocks, and Froggatt Edge are reproduced here in almost exaggerated form. Geologists say that the rock is the Chatsworth or escarpment grit, which cleaves into abrupt and angular masses whose outlines are not subdued to the rounded forms of the Kinder Scout grit. The traveller on the once-important coach road from Buxton sees glowering above him, on Ramshaw Edge, a grotesque succession of ghoulish faces, bovine and porcine heads, and half-finished monsters springing from the parent rock. And beyond, where Hen Cloud extends its array of pinnacles, he sees still more impossible shapes set in stone, outlines that the camera may prove to be less than vertical or only slightly overhanging, but to the eye appear like curving horns, their points overweighted with threatening tons of rock.

On Hen Cloud is to be found the pick of the climbing. It is as shapely and dignified a summit as any 3,000ft. sgurr in the Western Highlands; its long ridge bristles with sharp teeth, and the noble cliff fronting it is as imposing in contour, as seen against the clouds, as if its extreme height of 150ft. or so were magnified fourfold. We will tackle the most prominent of this handsome set of teeth as a first trial of what the Staffordshire sgurr can offer in the way of problems. It is not a considerable climb—quite the reverse—yet not too easy. Let us call it a tussle with the gloves on. For if, as is likely, the stony giant knocks you backwards, there is a thick pad of heather to fall on, with deep cushions of peat below. We get up by means of a winding fissure which allows the hands a good grip at the bottom, and, when the corner gets too rounded for that, permits the arm to be thrust in to secure a friction - hold. This sort of thing makes careful balancing a necessity. As we transfer our weight so as to get a pull sideways, we suddenly find we have lost what grip we had and tumble back into the heather. Jumping up for a second round, we attack again with more science, and, puffing and blowing, we get a higher grip, and bestride the giant's shoulders right underneath his colossal head. The descent on the other side is quite easy.

A hundred yards further on the continuous wall of Hen Cloud begins, flanked with tiers of ruined cliff that offer ways up of every grade of difficulty. There are virgin climbs here still, only waiting the arrival of a competent party; the mould and vegetation clinging to every chink shows, at all events, that they have not been ascended since days that we may now count prehistoric. The climbs that we accomplish are decidedly hard, and in most cases would be dangerous without a discreet employment of the rope. The face is uniformly steep, only a shade out of the vertical, and the holds are small and far apart. One face-climb looked possible, where we worked up some broken rocks in a sort of incipient gully; but half-way up we found the next move impracticable and gave it up. It would be tiresome to catalogue every one of the climbs that we discovered on Hen Cloud and on the great mass of crags over against us, Roach End. One gritstone chimney is remarkably like another; the minute differences are to be relished only by the connoisseur. Gullies with long strides where the happy scrambler holds on to a scratch in the wall whilst he passes from one toe-scrape to the next, chock-stones of the most varied construction, windy corners where he trusts his salvation to a finger-grip whilst he hangs over the exposed face—he can revel in these and a profusion of equally charming problems to his heart's content.

Then we cross the saddle to Roach End, another peak of strange shape that appears to be a loose accumulation of boulders of all sizes and the most extravagant forms, gnarled, rifted, fantastically weathered, and often perched in situations that seem to defy the laws of mechanics. One enormous mass projects like a natural roof over the artificial roof of Rock Hall, a cottage built in the cliff, with a front of ashlar, and rooms partly hewn out and partly shaped by nature in the rock. The natural chamber, now forming a sort of back kitchen, has an interesting history. Before the cottage was built, a score or two of years ago, it was lived in for nearly a century by a woman, Bess Bowyer, who was the daughter of a noted moss-trooper, " Bowyer of the Rocks," once the terror of this neighbourhood. She

herself was by no means a law-abiding person, for the
eccentricities of her dwelling place enabled her to shelter
smugglers, deserters, and other malefactors, and to
outwit the authorities with success and impunity. A
handsome girl, who passed as her daughter, was a still
more romantic inmate of this weird habitation. She is
said to have been heard often of a summer night singing
in an unknown tongue among the crags. At last she
was carried off by strange men, and the old crone was
left disconsolate, afterwards being found dead in the
cave she had lived in so long.

The gigantic projection of the cliffs that seems to
be threatening instant destruction to Rock Hall, nestling
underneath, is, I believe, called the Raven Rock. Some
villagers of Upper Hulme, who saw us returning from
the fray, were anxious to know if we had scaled this
imposing crag, which they evidently considered the
finest climb about here, and were much disappointed
to learn we had not attempted it. The rustic being no
climber himself, thinks nothing of impossibilities; or,
rather, he thinks everything else unworthy of a professed
cragsman's skill. Even our arboreal ancestors would
have been puzzled to climb the Eagle Rock, and we
shall never be equal to it until our constitution has been
reconstructed on the angelic plan. Not far away is a
rock inscribed with a record of the Duke and Duchess of
Teck's visit to the Roaches.

Until recently, one acquired the freedom of the whole
wild domain of the Roaches for a summer's day on
disbursing the sum of twopence sterling at Rock Hall.
But a fit of insanity indulged in by some trippers who
set a moor on fire has forced the proprietor to impose
great restrictions on the public. So the many are fined
for the silly exploits of a few. The ridge extends along
the Staffordshire border to the forest walls of the Dane's

deep glen, on the slope high above which is situated
the extraordinary chasm of Ludchurch. And the walk
between Ludchurch and Rock Hall is exceedingly
fine. The rugged escarpment overlooks a strip of
delicious wildwood and brake, where you walk knee-
deep in fern and bilberry, ling and heather-bells; great
rocks are flung at random among the pines and larches,
and there is only one thing to long for, a drink of water,
for there are no springs. One hot summer's day, three
of us who had been scrambling all the morning on
Roach End and were parched with thirst, came suddenly
on a little tarn, high up behind the edge, called
the Doxy Pool. Its waters were peaty-brown, but
clear; it was brim full, and the very picture of coolness.
We could not resist the temptation, and two of us
plunged in. At first, we found the bottom clear and
sandy, and the water fairly deep; but, incautiously, we
struck out for the middle, and the result was dreadful
and astonishing. Out there the bottom was spongy, and
seemed to be covered with an oozy accumulation of
decayed peat, which, on being stirred up, discharged a
violent odour, as if some noisome explosive had gone
off. We swam and floundered back with headlong
haste to the sandy beach where we had waded in; and
I think we must have used up all the clean water that
remained in the little mere in washing off the traces of
this grimy misadventure. So prompt were our movements that the camera man failed entirely to get a
permanent record of the incident.

I was most impressed by the Roaches in a solitary
walk along the cliff-top one summer's evening. It was
evening indeed on one side, where the high crest of the
hills cast a shadow far across the gloomy moorlands
towards the bare eastern hills that roll monotonously
away to the valley of the Dove and the Manifold. On

this side it was unutterably dreary; but in the west it
was still afternoon, for the sun shone above the Staffordshire and Cheshire hills, and, instead of dun moorlands
relieved only with white acres of cotton-grass and the
black, gaunt shapes of the tors, I looked over fat
pastures and well-timbered agricultural lands to the
smoky haze of the industrial regions. It was just the
same contrast as presents itself continually in Derbyshire—the jagged edge and the soft curves of the dale,
the freedom and deep quiet of the moor, and the din
of a thousand workshops, thought of, if not heard, in
the hazy distance.

XVII.

ALPORT CASTLES.

ALPORT CASTLES is one of those rare bits of scenery that the tourist never finds out, and that are often unknown even to the inquisitive pedestrian. Hid away in the remote valley of the Alport, a mile or so above its junction with Ashop Dale, it is quite off the beaten track, and, unless the road to Castles Farm is a right of way, which I doubt, there is not even a distant point accessible from which its strange configuration of cloven hillside can be seen. Years before I had visited the desolate defile of the Alport, as already described in these pages; but then we were for many hours wrapped up in a blinding mist, and saw next to nothing of the Castles.

Once upon a time—it may be centuries and more than centuries ago—an extraordinary landslip took place here, something like the landslip that originated the Ludchurch ravine, although the resulting conformation is entirely different. The shale grit is liable to these disasters, the foundations being too weak to hold up the superstructure, which topples over or shifts bodily down the hill, as it came to pass here.

Walking up the valley, which speedily grows as wild as any dale or clough in the whole of Peakland, you notice that the hill to the right appears to have been violently shaken. A disorderly array of knolls and crags are flung down its sides, but are grass-grown and shaggy with scattered trees, the scars healed over by the lapse of ages. As we approach the farmstead, the sole habitation in the valley, like some clachan in a forlorn highland glen, we observe proofs more recent and undisguised of a mighty catastrophe on the hillside. The ground covered by Castles Wood is all broken and convulsed, whilst for many furlongs the lofty edge of Birchinlee Moor has had its rocky foundations exposed by some enormous force. The long sheer cliff that remains as a gigantic scar, testifying to this ancient event, straight and even as a fortress wall, has been named the Castles by imaginative dalesmen. From the foot of the cliff, the wreckage has rolled down the slopes in tumultuous heaps and mounds, bearded with copse and stunted trees.

I was looking for the salient rock that the men of the Peak have called the Tower, and for a while I did not distinguish it, not knowing exactly what to look for. Then as I came right under the broken hill, I saw a dark and rugged shape gradually outline itself against the dark precipice. Here was the Tower, then, a long pinnacled ridge, a solid strip torn from the face of the hill, sharp as a knife-edge and jagged as a piece cut from a Coolin peak. Going through the farmyard and a little way up the bare valley, I crossed the great litter of boulders and shingle flung at random by the Alport in its winter fury, and took my way up through the ragged wood. This way the detached ridge presents its end as a slender peak, with a steep grassy shoulder leading up to it. Whatever the date of the landslip, the ground is still scooped out into undrained hollows; there has not been time for definite watercourses to be produced. Clambering up from rock to rock, I reached the peak hand-over-hand. The cone of solid grit has been shivered to the base by the power that tore it away, huge blocks are tumbled down the slopes on either hand, others are wedged or hang precariously on its flanks, waiting to be loosened for another roll downhill. From the peak a thin curtain of rock extends across the hillside, parallel to the Castles, with a perpendicular face of about a hundred feet facing those tiers of clean-cut walls and terraces of crumbling shale, across a deep basin piled up with fragments. To the right a savage ravine goes up towards the hill-top. Altogether it is like a wild corrie in the Grampians. Even now the havoc is proceeding. Reddish heaps of *débris* have fallen newly among the black, weather-beaten ruins; the scars are fresh, and numberless masses are evidently on the point of giving way.

After a scramble on the steep corners and fissures of the ridge, I clambered down into the hollow and up to the main cliff, which appeared to have one vulnerable point right in the middle. Anywhere else, the climber would venture at his peril among the tottering masses of undercut rock. I rested and ate my lunch before making my way up the cliff. No glimpse of house or road or footpath was to be had here. The solitary farm was hid by the Tower. Kinder's gloomy bulk seemed to close up the mouth of the valley, and in the other direction, the narrow clough threaded its way between hills whose vast forms seemed to be pushing together as if to strangle the little river, on its way down from the high moors about Bleaklow Head. I was surrounded by the sweeping curves of the great moorland hills, whose very simplicity of form and utter blankness gives them an incomparable majesty. The wind brushing the dry herbage, the homeless cry of the plover and curlew, the melancholy murmur of the river, and most of all the mists sliding stealthily and threateningly over the opposite hill, chilled one with a sense of being cut off and far removed from everything

human. When the cold creeping greyness stole into
the little corrie, right between me and the Tower, and
the whole world was shut out, no privacy could have
been more absolute than mine, alone in this hidden
cleft of the stormy hills. But there were miles to go
before I should see a house or a beaten track, and it
behoved me to hurry, if I would not be caught by the
mist on the moorlands between the Alport and the
Derwent. I scrambled up the lowest tier of rocks,
picking my way cautiously over the shaly terraces,
and found myself amid a confusion of tottering crags,
where every splinter and crevice must be tested ere I
put my weight upon it. One ponderous block held
firm whilst I pulled myself up to its level, then it slewed
round as if on a swivel; a push would have sent it
crashing among the wreckage under the cliff, but I
forbore. There is an awfulness about such a spot, when
you are alone, that I would not disturb so rudely.
Giving the dangerous block a wide berth, I crept
through more piles of disintegrated sandstone, and then
the steepness grew less, and I found myself on the
cliff-top and nearly on the crest of the hill.

My course now was very simple. I must keep along
the top of the moor as far as the head of some clough
leading down to the Westend River, where it flows
between the heights of Westend and Ronksley Moors
towards Derwent Dale, from that wild gathering-ground
of waters under Bleaklow, one of the earth's waste
places. Care must be taken not to descend inadvertently either into Alport Clough on the one hand, or
into Ouzleden Clough on the other; such a mistake
would be impossible in clear weather, but absurd things
happen in the mist. So I kept on about a mile, and
then began to follow the water downhill, till the ground
grew hollow and it was plain that I had come to the

I

head of Fagney Clough, which drains into the Westend. I shook off the last faint streamers of mist, just as a deep, brake-covered ravine opened beneath me, with the woods of Westend Clough at the mouth of it. A struggle through dense brake and a run downhill brought me to the door of Westend Farm, whence I caught a parting glimpse, up the trackless river dale, of the forlorn region of Featherbed Mosses and mist-haunted hills, before rounding the bend where Derwent Dale comes at last into view.

XVIII.

A FEW LIMESTONE SCRAMBLES IN DERBY- SHIRE AND LEICESTERSHIRE.

ALTHOUGH the grit of Derbyshire and the neighbourhood abounds in excellent practice scrambles, the limestone escarpments, often much higher and quite as extensive, furnish us with very few. We have here two sorts of limestone, the unaltered carboniferous or mountain limestone and the dolomitised or magnesian; the latter is a famous rock in the estimation of mountaineers, for it is the material of which the incomparable Dolomites are constructed. The wide tracts of mountain limestone produce scenery that is familiar to every tourist, whilst the dolomite is found only in fragments here and there. Nevertheless, an insignificant outcrop of dolomite offers more climbing than all the grandly-named limestone crags in all the dales. The rock steeples of Dovedale, painted and photographed by thousands of admirers, have attracted many a cragsman from afar. These apostolic colossi have something of the awful charm of the cathedral climbs with which certain illustrious scramblers began their careers. But those rock-climbers who look on scenery as a bore have all been thoroughly disappointed with Dovedale.

Twice with a party of friends I have made attempts to climb the great fissure that splits the High Tor at Matlock from crown to base. The interior of this chasm is not unlike the fissures to be found in the Peak Cavern and the Speedwell Mine, or such sub-aerial openings as Elden Hole. Probably its origin was not very different. We scrambled down steep slopes of clay and scree for nearly a hundred feet, at which point we came to the first of a series of bridges formed of great blocks that had tumbled athwart the cleft. From bridge to bridge we cautiously made our way till we reached a gap of some 20ft., the stones that we shifted in our movements crashing all the while into the black gulf beneath us, whose depth we could not ascertain. I will not predict that nobody will be found daring enough to clamber, with the aid of a rope, from one gigantic chockstone to the next, but the dark, cave-like aspect of the dismal place took from us any desire to attempt the feat. Our efforts to enter the gully at the foot were likewise a failure, but not so decisive as to take away all hopes of doing it. A little engineering might perhaps enable us to reach the first landing.

There is one climb on this rock that many cragsmen would certainly call a good one, whilst others would denounce it as dangerous, rotten, and illegitimate. This is the "Dargai," in Cave Dale at Castleton. Peveril's keep looks down on the bend in the dale where the crack splits the sheer cliff from top to bottom, but you must come down into the ravine to see the climb itself. It was on a bleak, overcast morning that the discoverer introduced three of us to this desperate little climb. We were extremely hungry after a walk over the limestone uplands, and flatly refused to be victimised. So we went to the Peak Hotel and ate a sumptuous lunch, after which our inexorable leader drove us out, full of meat and sloth, back to the "Dargai." It is a climb that few men would try unroped. My acquaintance with its rickety joints and deceptive holds was made in a shower of fine rain that rendered it more slippery than ever; wet limestone is abominable stuff. The first ten feet or so are easy. We mount into a recess with a sort of old-fashioned chimney extending over it, which dwindles presently to a crack. One's troubles begin about the middle. Here the crack is too narrow to let you jam yourself in, and as for gripping the edge—why, the edge comes off in lumps unless you handle it gingerly. But the crack serves to steady one if the tiny ledges are used with caution. Then comes the last part and the worst. Midway in the final pitch a sapling sprouts from the cliff. Now, according to the laws, written and unwritten, of the climber's art, this harmless vegetable must on no account be touched. But it is right in the way, and to make the difficulty of avoiding it greater its lithe trunk offers the only accessible hold for several feet. It would be " a touch beyond the reach of art " to leave it alone, so we fling scruples to the winds and push our way through the foliage up to the cliff's brow, where the gratified proprietor of the " Dargai " shakes each arrival by the hand.

I know only one finer climb on mountain limestone, and that is far away in Somerset, in Burrington Combe, where a mighty rib of the Mendips affords a clean scramble of 250ft. At Cheddar and Ebbor, in the same quarter, there are magnificent displays of sheer rock, but hardly any climbs are to be found; the limestone ledges always seem to be turned upside down, and every face is either too easy for sport or absolutely impossible. Let us be off, then, to the Dolomites.

A capital series of climbs on magnesian limestone exists at Breedon - on - the - Hill, on the borders of Leicestershire and Derbyshire, where an isolated mass of this rock looks across the Trent Valley towards the hills of the Peak and was occupied as a military post in Roman times and by an Austin priory in the middle ages. The "Bulwark" hangs, like the fort on Mam Tor, right on the edge of the cliff; parts, indeed, of the rampart and fosse have been destroyed by the aggressions of a quarrying company. How much of the picturesque scarp that rises in places to a height of 250ft. owes its present form to past lime-burners and how much to natural causes it is hard to say, so well has nature disguised the ravages of man. But the natural crags are fairly extensive, whilst excellent scrambles are to be found on rocks that have certainly not been sculptured by weather alone. Sgurr-na-Breedon, an outlying peak, doomed, alas! to perish in the not distant future by the quarryman's blast, is partly natural, partly artificial. Had you seen it in July, when its sides and shoulders were a blaze of wallflowers, growing in such profusion and variety of colour and shade as any lover of gardens would have envied, you would not have deemed that this semi-artificial origin detracted from its comeliness. I have tried the mettle of Sgurr-na-Breedon after stern days on Great Gable, on the peaks of Skye, and on the climbs of Glencoe, and was far from feeling that I had exchanged work for mere play.

One of the most eminent authorities on rock-climbing once observed to me that the characteristic of our Derbyshire climbs is that they are extremely technical. At Breedon we have an epitome of all the *technique* of crag-work except the points special to chimneys and gullies. The scale is small, of course; but then if you have a smaller distance to fall the holds also are smaller, so that matters are somewhat equalised. Then, again, beyond a certain height, something less than a hundred feet, the consequences of a fall do not increase in gravity; wherefore the wise climber may,

Photo by   *G.A. Fowkes, Derby.*

THE DESCENT PERILOUS, BREEDON.

EAST ARÈTE, BREEDON.

Photo by   *G.A. Fowkes, Derby.*

EAST CLIMB, BREEDON.

if he please, enjoy nearly all the delights of his sport on quite a minor height, including those possibilities of sudden death that we pretend, by a pleasant convention, to find so alluring. The Sgurr has at present three sporting ways to the summit. The top part of one has been blown away by recent blasting; still, the best things will probably wear for a few more seasons. The climb nearest the " Nose " was considered impracticable till, one day recently, I tested the lower holds and was tempted on and on until I found myself hanging on a smooth cliff by the tips of my fingers, and realised that, without eyes behind me, getting down was a worse venture than going up. Thus it came about that the " Nose " was climbed, and one other day, to please an exacting photographer, I did it again; but such risks might well be reserved for peaks of greater fame. Hard by, a friend was nearly carried away by a big stone that he dislodged accidentally, for the rock here is not dolomitised to such an extent as that at Harborough and Brassington, and, consequently, is by no means so trustworthy. Two or three sharp *arêtes* converge towards the Low Man (the High Man was recently beheaded), and thence a few years ago a sensational traverse might have been enjoyed along the knife-edge of the " Crib," where one assumed the most delightfully insane positions in wriggling along, with a hundred-foot drop to left and right, up to the hill-top, a hundred yards away. Unhappily, this fine landmark has been at length attacked, through a change in the ownership, and the " Crib " is gradually being burned in the kilns. A shattered cliff traversed by the " Descent Perilous " overlooks a deep hollow, that has been left for so many decades to the weather and the kindly influences of vegetation as to deserve its fanciful title, the " Corrie "—the names here are polyglot, combining

Welsh and Gaelic reminiscences. The pinnacled buttress, or "fiacaill," as the Highlanders would call it, at the side of the Corrie is too steep half-way up to be climbed. Beyond it there is some first-rate scrambling on *arêtes* and faces. From below the rocks appear to be well broken, and the first few steps are seductively easy. Then comes an area of open cliff where the apparent ledges prove to be meagre crannies filled with dirt and plumed with grass-tufts, with wallflowers and purple snapdragons, where a hobnail can find hardly anything to bite on. Once or twice, novices who had been tempted to ascend as far as the little cave a few feet up have been unable to move either up or down till the leader crept round to a point right over their heads, and brought them out with an unceremonious pull on the rope. The place abounds in striking situations. From the mimic precipices, peaks, and crags we look far over a beautiful country of woods and fields towards the peaky hills of Charnwood Forest, crested with volcanic rocks. To the left is the active volcano of Coalville, with the fumaroles of a dozen pits vomiting smoke. And down at the foot of Sgurr-na-Breedon the quarry-men, agile fellows, who work for days in hazardous places, stand looking at us with open mouths, marvelling at such unpaid daring.

There is an outcrop of dolomite belonging to the Permian epoch on the border-line of Derbyshire and Nottinghamshire, at Cresswell, with a gorge cut through it leading into the domain of Welbeck Abbey. This wooded gorge is very pretty, with its long and narrow mere lying between the rugged buttresses of limestone, which are hollowed out into dark dens and caves, and heavily mantled with ivy, brushwood, and trees. Its suddenness, too, as you approach it from the level and monotonous coal country, is very striking. Cresswell is famous for the great quantities of pleistocene remains found there some years ago, for these caves were the lairs of wild beasts and wild men at a remote geological period. There is a railway station hard by, but we reached the crags by a ten-mile drive from Mansfield—a drive through a howling wind in November. We had been told to expect some scrambling, but we were disappointed, only finding a few climbs of an indefinite and unsatisfactory character. On the south side of the mere, however, where a long stretch of corrugated and weathered cliff rises vertically to a height of a hundred feet, I ascended some twenty-five feet of what looked like a good climb, somewhat sensational, but apparently just feasible. But it was raining and blowing, and this sort of limestone gets peculiarly greasy and intractable in such weather, so the climb was left unfinished for any future scrambler who may chance to visit this picturesque spot.

XIX.

THE BRASSINGTON AND HARBOROUGH DOLOMITES.

WITHIN reach of a pleasant walk from the Stride, and of a rather dreary but shorter one from the Black Rocks near Cromford, are the Brassington and the Harborough Rocks, two considerable outcrops of dolomitised limestone belonging to the Carboniferous period. The most direct way to the Harborough Rocks is along the line of the High Peak Railway, if the authorities will allow you to use it. Scarcely three miles away from the Black Rocks a flattish hill rises above the dismal grey landscape, with what appear in the distance like terraces and walls of gleaming limestone crossing its front in fairly regular lines. On a nearer view these are found to be broken up into crags and needles, all very steep, if not actually vertical. Their fronts look too much like smooth walls, until one gets close enough to see that the face of the rock is eroded into innumerable little holes and crevices, making it look like the outside of a sponge or some species of coral. These, though small, offer such trusty holds for fingers and hobnails that one may walk with tolerable ease right up a perpendicular face, and give a spectator the idea that one is using Mr. H. G. Wells's contrivance for annihilating gravity. They must, however, be handled with care, for they are often worn so thin and frail as to break away like pieces of biscuit.

The best scramble is in the middle of the range of crags, on a crocketed pinnacle that just overtops the sky-line. A ledge bisecting the *arête* gives a desirable rest before we attack the steep upper part, where holds are few and small. The best way is to get right on the corner, and climb as if it were a post, gripping it with legs and arms. But the grips near the top are sound, and give one a delightful pull up to the corrugated summit. Every yard of rock to left and right offers a climb of some kind or other, and a small chimney hard by is equipped with an ideal chock-stone, one of those pattern specimens that occur so rarely, save in the illustrations to a book on the calisthenics of climbing. The farmer came on the scene one morning, we thought at first to admire our performances, but he proved to be rather an exacting critic, for he told us that two Alpine climbers had been here lately and shown him some extraordinary feats of derring-do. This put us on our mettle, and we essayed to prove ourselves not unequal to most of the things done by these men of renown. But after he had thoroughly taken the wind out of us, he led the way to the stiffest climb of all, a narrow, inconspicuous fissure, twisting up a corner of the cliff. It looked innocent and inoffensive enough. We scouted the idea of being worsted; but, alack! we were tired. This was our second innings that day, for we had walked across from the Black Rocks, and this little climb demands fresh muscles as well as strong. Gripping the thin edge of the fissure, I levered myself up a few feet, and jammed the left arm and leg well in, pawing wildly with my right for some dent or wrinkle in the smooth wall. I wriggled up inch by inch till I could all but clutch a safe little hold near the top; then my arms gave out, and I was extremely glad of a friendly shoulder to help me back to mother earth. The dolomite steeple that crowns the escarpment a few yards off is a more satisfactory climb. The ledge dividing it into two storeys is broad enough to be called a terrace, and forms a suitable platform whence to attack the difficult upper stage. A sharp corner goes up from this take-off, straight and ledgeless to the top, its sides very smooth. Only by embracing this narrow corner, so as to make use of some tiny nicks and wrinkles with a sideways pull, can one master it at all.

Our yeoman friend took us to see a little cave among the rocks, which, so he informed us, had been a hermit's cell in the times of the Druids. To confirm this remarkable theory, he stated that an incised crucifix used to be traceable on the walls. A rocking-stone is, of course, quite an ordinary appurtenance of Druidical shrines, and, sure enough, there was the Rocking-Stone in front of the entrance. In shape and size it is like a small tower, slightly tapering. It rests unstably on one end, which is flanged. By a stout effort one can induce it to rock slightly, very slightly; but that is more than the Logan and several other celebrated rocking-stones can perform to justify their fame. There are remains of a weather-cock at the top.

The wan greys and greens of the limestone uplands that stretch away westward from the heathery region of the grit are dull and woe-begone to the eye; the landscape is wild and lonely without any touch of grandeur, and the chimneys of the derelict power-stations on the mineral line, with the refuse piles of mines and quarries strewn here and there—patches of sheer ugliness—disattune the mind to the sweeter melancholy that bareness and austerity awaken. It was like a foretaste of Dovedale when we came over the next hill-brow and looked down upon the pastoral combe,

Photo by   G.A. Fowkes, Derby.

THE LONG CLIMB AT BRASSINGTON ROCKS.

Photo by   Guy D. Barton.

CRACK CLIMBING AT BRASSINGTON.

CRACK AT BRASSINGTON.

Photo by   Claude Barton.

A FACE CLIMB AT BRASSINGTON.

dappled with wood and spinney, where the Brassington rocks crown a brace of dolomite tors. The spot is an oasis in a desert. One side of the higher tor is carved into three enormous stairs—three cliffs with terraces between. On the slopes, on the terraces, and on the summit, flourishes a huge tangle of trees, bushes, and flowers, half-concealing the ruggedness of the crags. It is one of the choicest hunting-grounds in Derbyshire for the botanical collector; there is, to my knowledge, only one better spot for rare plants, a haunt of quietness and ancient peace that the tourist has completely over-looked, nor am I going to direct him thither.

The principal climb starts at the foot of the lowest stair. In front is a splintered mass of dolomite, cloven into a sheaf of spires and pinnacles. We climbed the thin edge of one of these to a shelf, where a choice of routes presented itself—a short chimney, a crinkled face, and another thin, knife-like edge. We took the last. It led us, with some stiff toe-and-finger work, to the top of a square block, islanded amid the luxuriant jungle. Across a gap, we saw a big smooth buttress emerge, gleaming white amid the verdure. This led to the foot of a superb rock-tower, a beautiful piece of limestone architecture, loftier in shape and dignity than in actual height. Though but a salient buttress of the terrace that lies under the topmost band of rocks, the stately pinnacle seemed to crown the whole rugged pile of hoary crags and bosky slopes, its white head in the blue almost over our heads. Could we climb it? The sides were vertical or overhanging; nothing could look worse to a climber who knew not the benevolent nature of dolomite. First I tried the straight wall in front, and crept up from chink to chink, resting all on my fingers, and hardly finding a toe-scraper for my feet. Then the rock bulged slightly, and the finger-holds grew thin and brittle. Unfortunately, we had not got a rope, and the jagged splinters under the herbage below is distressing stuff to fall upon; I thought it hardly justifiable to go ahead, although there were a few nail-marks about, showing that the aforementioned Alpine climbers had been there. We adopted a less exposed course at the side and, reaching the big terrace, looked across to the uppermost wall of crag. Still keeping conscientiously to the line of our scramble, though it is easy at any point to shirk the main diffi-culties, we had to choose between another short *arête* and a curious chimney. We selected the former, and, at the top of it, strode across to a steep rib that carried us to the summit of the tor.

All round is a picturesque jumble of dells and knolls, woody in spots, and raked with terraces of grey crag, among which a slim pinnacle or two sticks out, tempting morsels to the climber-up of unconsidered trifles. The wide terrace beneath is covered with an almost impenetrable brake, even the unarmed wild-flowers conspiring with rank nettles and thistles, brambles and thorn-bushes, to keep out intruders; whilst the floor is a regular trap, deep holes and channels and sharpened splinters, gins powerful enough to break a man's leg, lurking beneath the dense herbage. From spring to autumn there is a glowing succession of colour—colour in great masses—all about the shattered walls and turrets. In the spring it is chiefly blues and whites, bluebells and whitethorn, colours of exquisite purity that give way as summer advances to more copious tints and wilder magnificence. Towering bell-flowers and filmy cranesbill, with their different blue; creamy meadowsweet and pink valerian, mingling their fragrant essences; and rich purple clumps of that rare bloom, the orpine, bask in the sun. Among the rocks, in shadier places, grow a multitude of various ferns, delicate spleenworts and wall rue in the crannies of the dolomite; hart's tongue, polypodies, and different shield ferns on the ground; ivy cleaves to the rocks; ropes and tangles of clematis and woodbine are flung at random from tree to pinnacle. Yet there are breadths of naked crag, such as the beetling wall to the west of the scramble I have just described. It is like a palisade built of tall, straight megaliths, cleanly hewn and smooth but for the infinitesimal roughnesses of the surface. The cliffs of the other tor have the same columnar structure, which affords an extraordinary variety of climbing, backing-up, finger-work, and, most curious and characteristic of all, fly-walking across perpendicular slabs, that appear at a few yards' distance to be perfectly bare of holds.

One may spend a long summer's day on the Brassington and Harborough Rocks, if one can afford to be content with small problems, full of change and always interesting. A mile away is the homely village of Brassington, cosily placed under the sheltering hills, old-fashioned and unspoiled, because it is so far from railways and the haunts of tourists. But old-fashioned delights have drawbacks to correspond, and two of us will not readily forget the blending of full-flavoured odours that was wafted, by the opening of a door, into the room where we had tea, the easiest scents to recognise coming from cheese-press and pig-sty respectively. There is a pleasant downhill road to the nearest railway station at Wirksworth.

XX.

THE HEMLOCK STONE, NEAR NOTTINGHAM.

THE environs of Nottingham seem an unlikely place for climbing, unless one went as far as Sherwood Forest and tried some of those gnarled and weathered oaks, with rinds rough and hard almost as granite, which ought surely to offer better sport than the poplars recommended lately by a mountaineering journal. But, four miles from the market-place of Nottingham, there stands on the side of a hill a singular block of sandstone that affords very good practice. The top of this rock had been saturated with calcareous deposits, and when the surrounding strata of soft sandstone was eroded away, it was left towering on a pedestal much smaller than the hardened cap. Hence the extravagant shape of the Hemlock Stone, which, it is only too obvious, cannot stand in its present top-heavy condition much longer, but must inevitably go rolling down the hill some frosty morning.

Since every stage in the little climb is by overhanging ledges, much neat gymnastic work is to be had here. The first move is to reach a horizontal shelf crossing the longest face; but as the rock beneath it has been weathered away, leaving a hollow, this looks quite inaccessible. We arrived there one rainy morning, and took shelter under the stone umbrella, while we discussed the problem before us. So greasy and

Photo by   G.A. Fowkes, Derby.

THE NOTCH CLIMB – HEMLOCK STONE.

absurdly impossible did the thing look that our courage was as damp as our clothes. Perhaps a lowland pinnacle, only 30ft. high, seems hardly worth much fuss; but, after all, the ordinary way up Scawfell Pinnacle is not longer, and is incomparably easier. After several athletic attempts to get up at one end or the other, a tiny crevice was descried, which could be reached by a scramble up some ledges, and used for steadying purposes by one hand whilst the other clutched the bracket supporting the horizontal shelf. Next, swinging off clear, with arms flung round the projecting bracket and knees drawn up underneath, we get hold of a knob just over the shelf and the first man had arrived. My hand bore scars for a long while to remind me of a friend, weighing thirteen or fourteen stone, who fell on the rope just here, and squeezed my flesh against the sharp-grained surface of the rock. The shelf half encircles the Hemlock Stone, broadening out at one end under the still ampler top, so that we are comfortably dry while our friends are downstairs in the rain. But how is that projecting roof overhead to be escaladed? Creeping round till the shelf dwindles to nothing, we observe a gap in the eaves, where the top projects only for a foot or two. One of us cautiously holds the rope upon a slight projection, a poor and doubtful sort of belay, hoping that in case of a slip the falling man will be pulled up somehow, and only swing a dozen feet or so against the unpadded rock; and now the leader leans outwards and feels for hand-hold. For a moment his feet continue to graze the rock, while he gropes about for something trusty to clutch; then he lays hold higher up, his body swings out, and now he must pull up with might and main over the rugosities of the roof. A starling had its nest in a crevice at the " Notch," as this gap in the defences

J

is called, showing that there is not much traffic that way.

But, on coming again, we found there were two other ways of getting over the projecting roof from the traverse, and at least two different ways of reaching the traverse from the ground. One of these, the easy finish, is at the far end, and by no means an obvious route to find. You crawl or scramble or go as you please, along the horizontal shelf aforesaid, which is very narrow, and overhung in a most uncompromising manner by the upper part of the stone; and, on reaching the end, you clamber round it, and the rest is easy. The " Notch " climb, which is very dangerous, is almost forgotten now. It has been done very rarely since, and hardly at all without a rope from the top.

However, the summit is not likely to become a popular resort, although many an urchin has got as high as the broad shelf roofed over by the top, a place large enough for a picnic party of moderate size; but some time ago, our party discovered a tin box, fixed recently in a crack on the summit, which contained the cards of some ambitious scramblers, who were evidently under the impression that they had captured a virgin peak. The box disappeared mysteriously a little later. Whether it enfolded the name of a daring person who reached the top, but was so prostrated by the consciousness of his dizzy altitude that he had to be carried down with ropes and ladders, is another mystery of the Hemlock Stone.

The third route to the top is by way of the vertical fissure that rises immediately above us after attaining the shelf by the method already described. It is quite as dangerous as the " Notch," and I mention it only to warn against using it without a rope from above. A certain young friend of mine, anxious to do the climb and ignorant of any other possible way, took this obvious one, and by sheer strength and determination forced himself up. Nobody will be surprised to hear that another of his exploits was to fall backwards down a cliff 40ft. high; without, however, sustaining any damage or getting killed, an incident that he is perhaps reserving for more august conditions. Another feat of peculiar daring was performed by an unroped climber, who made his way right round the crag, a few feet below the top. Without abating one jot of my admiration for these displays of prowess, I can hold them up conscientiously only as fearful examples.

XXI.

EXPLORING ELDEN HOLE.

"BE you going up to see the Hole, gen'lemen?"
The question fell from the knot of quarrymen,
the driver of a shaky four-wheeler, and sundry
other loiterers, as we came shouldering our rücksacks
across the bridge at Peak Forest Station, where the
Derbyshire branch of the Midland Railway reaches its
summit-level of nearly a thousand feet above the sea.
Locally at all events, we thought, Elden Hole has not
fallen away from its old reputation, confirmed by
centuries of county historians, as one of the far-famed
Wonders of the Peak. Gaping, black and cavernous,
in the brow of a conspicuous hill, this strange, waterless
rift has from aboriginal times puzzled beholders and
begotten all sorts of myths. It was explored in 1873
by Mr. Rooke Pennington, author of " Barrows and
Bone Caves," who wrote a brief account of what he had
seen. But the narratives of the few earlier explorers
are mainly a sensational mixture of fact and fancy
that cannot now be separated. In Queen Elizabeth's
reign, it is related, the notorious Dudley, Earl of
Leicester, hired a peasant to be lowered into the chasm,
which was then believed to be bottomless. The episode
is incorporated by the philosopher Hobbes, author of
the " Leviathan," into his poem, " De Mirabilibus
Pecci," passages of which might have inspired Mr.
Rider Haggard's most appalling descriptions of strange
abysses and fabulous realms under the surface of the

earth. He says, for instance, of a piece of rock flung
into the Hole:—

> "The lowest deep descending, it broke through
>   Hell and the centre."

And in the same exaggerated strain he tells how the
hapless peasant, after descending "two hundred ells,"
was crazed by terror:—

> "He's drawn up; but, whether fear
> Immoderate distracted him, or 'twere
> From the swift motion as the rope might wreathe,
> Or spectrums from his dread, or hell beneath
> Frighted the wretch, or the soul's citadel
> Was stormed or taken by the imps of hell,
> For certain 'twas he rav'd; this his wild eyes,
> His paleness, trembling, all things verifies."

The poor man died in convulsions after eight days;
probably he had been knocked on the head by a falling
stone, or had collided with the rocky wall. Izaak
Walton's fellow-sportsman, the poet and savant, Charles
Cotton, says with reference to his attempt to measure
the depth:—

> "But I myself, with half the Peake surrounded,
> Eight hundred, fourscore and four yards have sounded."

Indeed, the vast discrepancies that have been handed
down to us in the recorded measurements can only be
accounted for on the supposition that the surveyors were
very mad or very anxious to keep up the reputation of
this local marvel, and therefore allowed the sounding
line to coil up on one of the ledges.

For our part we relied on Rooke Pennington's statement that the Hole is 180 feet deep. It is 200 feet deep
from the actual slope of the hill, while an inner cavern
descends 65 feet lower. Our object was not to
investigate myths, but to see if the Hole could be

descended by the ordinary methods used in rock-work. Rock-climbing above ground is fascinating sport; to enjoy it below the surface and in semi-darkness would surely be to catch a rarer thrill—at least, so we argued.

A walk of four miles, half the way to Castleton, brought us to the spot. From afar the black mouth of the Hole is plainly visible, an oblong rift, whose extreme length and width we found to be 111 feet and 18 feet respectively. For safety's sake a wall encircles it, a wall which is said to have had countless predecessors, for the first impulse of a visitor is to select a large stone and send it thundering into the depths, with the result that the floor at the bottom is piled with the ruins of walls built and rebuilt for many a century back. The steepness of the slope enhances the grandeur of this gateway to subterranean regions. On each side the bare walls descend sheer, with ferns and long grass, trailing masses of ivy, brambles and shrubs garlanding the rift. At the upper end there is a precipitous wall with giant blocks of limestone jutting out, as if a touch would hurl them headlong; but at the lower end the rocks are inclined somewhat, and we knew there would be excellent sport if we could make a way down such a staircase. We tossed for the privilege of descending as far as the rope would go, and the lot fell to a gentleman whose Norfolk suit had been much admired. With little help from us he climbed slowly to a sloping rock 70 feet down, called out that a few more feet of rope would enable him to see the bottom, and, as that was not forthcoming, he returned hand over hand. As soon as he came near enough for us to see that his new clothes were a mass of black slime from head to foot, our feelings of envy were much assuaged.

Six weeks later, in September, 1900, we were on the spot again with a party of seven experienced rock-climbers, and we had with us about 400 feet of Alpine Club rope. The gentleman who had suffered so wofully on the last occasion, Mr. A. L. Bagley, was allowed the honour of leading the way, and I came next, the first three men having about 80 feet of rope between each pair. One man remained at the top all day. Moving cautiously, one at a time, down the steep and slippery rocks, where the ordinary precautions used in crag-work had to be redoubled, we came at length to the sloping rock where our scout had previously stopped. Would it be possible to climb further was now the question, so as to let our men singly down the lowest pitch from a convenient shelf. The third man, Mr. Henry Bond, and I braced ourselves as firmly as we could on a steep slab coated with slippery mud, whilst Bagley attempted to climb along the ledges of the side wall. Suddenly, with a shout, he slipped off, swung in under our slab, which proved to be overhanging, and pulled Bond, who fortunately had a grip on my rope, four feet from his moorings before the party above could check him: for a few seconds the tension was alarming. And now, with muscles astrain, we let him down inch by inch into the shaft. When would he stop? we wondered anxiously, as the rope chafed through our burning hands and slipped over the edge out of sight. Hurrah! he had alighted somewhere, and none too soon, for my rope was paid out all but a foot or two. Peering over the edge while Bond steadied me, I caught a glimpse of Bagley perched in a niche, 70 feet below our lodgment and 30 feet from the bottom. We shouted the information to our friends higher up, and awaited their directions for the next move.

Resting in this precarious situation, we enjoyed a complete view of the high and rugged cliff that forms the upper end-wall of the cavity. Black masses of limestone seem piled above each other in regular courses; they overhang in places, and the heaps of rubbish that have accumulated on their upper edges look ready to pour into the Hole at the slightest disturbance. I was now instructed to go and relieve Bagley. Letting myself go over the brink, now in mid-air, now grazing the slippery walls, I dropped to the level of our leading man, who reached out a hand to draw me into the niche. Then carefully changing places with him, for the niche was too small to accommodate more than one saint, I shouted to those above to hold tight while I let my companion down single-handed. Now a longer pause occurred, while the party overhead were evidently discussing the situation. The job had proved much harder than had been anticipated, and it was a vital question now whether the hauling party of four, who were in a position of jeopardy, were capable of pulling a man up. They decided to test their powers by experiment, and word came for the man at the bottom to tie himself on, while I kept watch on the rope for fear of a hitch. Bagley was got up safely, but only with great expenditure of energy, and, this accomplished, they let me down the last pitch.

The bottom is an irregular oblong in shape, measuring 36 feet by 12 feet; the sloping floor is covered with broken rocks. It is a grim and gloomy spot, lighted by a very small patch of sky. Only parts of the great fissure extending skywards are visible, and all view of my comrades was cut off by overhanging ledges. On one side the floor falls away rapidly towards the mouth of a dark cave, which I resolved to explore while waiting for the next move of those above. Crawling under the low-browed portal, I found myself on a slope of thirty or forty degrees, covered with stones of all sizes in a very unstable condition. The

Photo by

H. Eggleston.

EXPLORING PARTY AT ELDEN HOLE.

air was good and my candle burned brightly, but its light was too feeble to reveal the extent of the lofty chamber into which I emerged. Keeping near the left wall, I crept down the slope, and in about 70 feet came to the farther wall of the cavern. A hole in the floor hard by seemed to point to an inner chamber, and fixing the candle between the stones I crawled in, but soon found there was not room for a human body to pass. Perhaps the hole is a mere water-sink; but it may possibly be connected with unexplored cavities. I now returned from the cave to the bottom of the Hole, just in time to see the lightest man of the party, Mr. F. Wightman, lowered over the last hundred feet. He barely touched the rocks anywhere, but, with a camera on his back, came down slowly, spinning like a piece of meat on a jack.

It now transpired that all hope had been abandoned of getting any more explorers down, the strain of pulling a man up a hundred feet sheer being too much for the party, fixed, as they were, in an awkward and dangerous situation. While we prepared to photograph our strange surroundings, they packed a Gladstone bag with electric lamps, paraffin, fireworks, and, most important of all, a supply of bottled drinks and sandwiches, which were badly needed, for several hours had elapsed since we left the surface of the globe. And disdaining squeamishness, with clothes wet with clay and mud, our hands, faces, and hair covered with dirt, and icy drops falling on us from the walls, we enjoyed a hasty lunch, and then proceeded into the cavern. So cold and humid was the atmosphere at the bottom of the Hole that the advent of a human body created a perceptible mist.

Our main object was to secure a view, but with only one man to hold the magnesium wire, we spent a considerable time in the cave to little profit. There is not a flat spot in the place; in the fitful light stumbles were frequent, and once the photographer, encumbered with camera, a torch, and a bottle of paraffin, slipped and let the camera roll down the stones. But we managed to illuminate the cavern magnificently with paraffin torches, magnesium, and Bengal fire. Within the low entrance a white arch, exquisitely symmetrical, soars high above our heads, as if to span the opening of some mighty chancel; and beyond, the walls of the great chamber ascend into a dome, the apex of which is hidden in darkness, but cannot be much less than a hundred feet high. We sent up a fire-balloon to a height of 50 feet, but it failed to reveal the farthest recesses of this weird roof. Everywhere the walls are encrusted with a massy growth of stalactites, some creamy-white, and sparkling with the reflections of our lamps; some brownish, fretted into a thousand wild shapes, which the shifting light seems to harmonise into vague designs, recalling the chiselled walls and vaulting of a cathedral. Water drips incessantly from the roof and trickles down the walls, but there is no spring or running water, though in one place, where we scrambled up a buttress at the side, we found the rocks water-worn, as if by an intermittent stream. The natives had warned us that the Hole would be full of water at the bottom; possibly a lake has been known to form, as has happened at Gaping Ghyll in Yorkshire; this would explain the presence of timber at the bottom of the cave. The chamber is interesting also, as showing how such waterless fissures as Elden Hole may perhaps have been formed. Disintegration of the limestone by means of acid-laden water is proceeding upwards, and in the course of ages may perhaps approach the surface, and make a new shaft. Such, at least, seems to be the theory adopted by Rooke Pennington. But Martel believes that Elden Hole is an old swallet; and I should be inclined to think that both this cavity and the shallower, but still considerable holes in the neighbourhood, such as Bull Pit and the cavity on Gautries Hill, engulfed streams at some far remote period, and were perhaps in direct communication with the water caverns at Castleton. To find the traditional passages through which the famous goose is said to have made its pilgrimage to the Devil's Hole, will, however, be a Herculean task, if ever undertaken, since the orifice will have been submerged beneath tons and tons of shattered limestone.

It was after 5 p.m. when we made our exit from the cave. Just as we emerged into the subdued daylight a big stone came hurtling down the chasm, bursting right in front, and sending a fragment whizzing between us. What were our comrades doing? We shouted to be drawn up, but could not make out what they shouted in reply, and not till afterwards did we get an explanation of what was going on aloft. They had been amusing themselves with scrambling on the upper end-wall, and when they received our summons were not ready to go to the top and descend the farther wall to our assistance. About 6 p.m. they began climbing down to their old lodgment, but dusk deepened rapidly into night at nearly a hundred feet from the surface, and to add to their difficulties the 400 feet of rope got into a hopeless tangle. Meanwhile our suspense was acute. Vainly we wondered what had taken place. Stones kept rattling down, but the length of the Hole made it possible to run for shelter between the sound of the first crash and their arrival at the bottom. Our combustibles had filled the place with smoke, the sting of which half blinded my companion. In an unlucky moment he put his hands into the bag, forgetting they were flavoured with paraffin; the lunch was rendered uneatable, and the pangs of hunger were added to the discomforts of our cold and miserable dungeon.

Soon after 7 o'clock, to our great relief, a shout came for Wightman, who, being light, was hauled up without serious difficulty, and I drew the rope back by means of a string attached to the end. Then the Gladstone bag and a rucksack were tied on and sent up, whilst I paid out the twine watchfully for fear of losing the rope. All at once I felt the string break, and somewhere up in the darkness the bags sounded as if they were jammed. Here was I with the last candle almost gone, and communication with the earth's surface apparently cut off until next day. But an accident occurred which was no misfortune—the bags caught in the rocks, and could not be pulled up. Various inexplicable sounds were wafted down the Hole, and presently there was a noise as of somebody descending, followed by a heavy thud. Striking a match, I saw that the luggage had returned, and after much shouting, I gathered that it was my duty to tie myself and the bags in a bundle to the rope, and be hauled up. The return journey was a trying one, both for those hauling this augmented load and for the battered victim, who, with rope round his chest, and with one heavy bag in front and another behind, choking respiration, swung to and fro in the dark and slimy pit, with hardly a ledge to rest foot or hand upon so as to give the hauling party a moment's relief. No wonder they described me as groaning all the way up; I was struggling for breath. Between my legs the bottom of the Hole was visible by glimpses, fitfully lighted by the last shred of cotton-wool soaked in paraffin; this dismal view receded slowly, as, with a cheery " Heave-ho! " the others hauled to the best of their powers.

About 8 o'clock I gripped hands with the nearest man, and the worst was over; yet nearly an hour elapsed before we got up the last pitches of the black funnel, where the big loose rocks had to be passed with utmost caution. Ah! what relief and what refreshment to step again into the open air! The wide hillside, the clear cold flood of moonlight, and the lakes of mist in the vale seemed never so beautiful as after our dreary imprisonment. I had spent all but nine hours below the ground, and Wightman had been with me the greater part of the time.

After such an experience it was a tame affair to descend the Hole in a " bosun's chair," yet to have succeeded in getting thirteen men to the bottom and up again without accident is a feat unique, so far as the pot-holes and caverns of the Pennine Chain are concerned; and, as the same methods were to be used in exploring the so-called " Bottomless Pit " in the Speedwell Mine, a brief account of the operations may be worth giving. The apparatus was simple, consisting chiefly of a stout cable crossing the rift, with a pulley or trolley running on it that could be held stationary at any point, while a rope about a hundred yards long ran over the wheel and supported a wooden seat. On Boxing Day, 1900, the usually deserted slope of Elden Hill presented a lively scene. Nearly twenty workers and volunteers were engaged with the tackle, and a crowd of villagers had gathered round, among them the parson from Peak Forest, genial and full of anecdote, and a farmer whose sire had gone down with Rooke Pennington in 1873, and whose long-cherished ambition we gratified by taking him down with us. Motley was our wear; one man was clothed in armour of new sacking, and many of our coats displayed the stains and tears acquired on our previous visit. Several vehicles drawn up on the rugged and roadless hillside showed the difficulty of conveying hither the piles of rope, stakes, tools, and multifarious appliances that lay about; a tent had been raised to shelter the telephone, and as a kitchen for preparing hot drinks and other refreshment.

Again we were behind time. The Sheffield and Castleton contingent were unfortunately delayed, and so retarded the work of the party. It had been proposed to use horse-power for hauling, but later on we had reason to congratulate ourselves on having sent away the horse, for the rope would certainly have got broken in some of our collisions with the rocks after dark. I was to have the honour of going down first. Swinging over the huge funnel, one could look down vertically 200 feet to the stony patch at the end of how strange a perspective! The novel point of view distorted everything. Now the tackle begins to creak, and away we go. The queer sensation is not unpleasant, and, with a life-line round one's body as a precaution, there is no danger. The journey seemed long and full of incident, the scenery not lacking in impressiveness and variety, yet it occupied only two and a half minutes. I was deposited in a heap on the steep slope, and at once signalled for the rope to be drawn up. Unfortunately the main rope and the life-line got entangled, and after each descent much time was consumed in unravelling the twist.

At length the creaking of the apparatus began again, warning me that another adventurer was on the way. The phenomenon now observed was rather puzzling; the man appeared to come round a corner at the top, and to descend at an angle of fifteen degrees from the perpendicular, and very odd he looked, with legs sticking out spiderwise, especially when the rope began to "twizzle." This slanting appearance showed what one would never suspect from the mere look of the place, that the shaft is considerably out of the vertical. The next man, who was burdened with the heavy telephone,

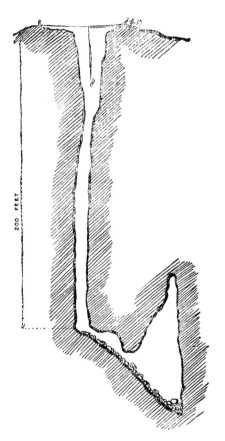

SECTIONAL DIAGRAM OF ELDEN HOLE.

By H. Arnold Bemrose, M.A., F.G.S.

suffered rather badly from the spinning. The instrument was now placed in a sheltered corner, and conversation began at once with the workers above ground. On the whole the telephone was very serviceable, but some curious dialogue enlivened us now and then. The Yorkshireman at the other end had a way of shouting at the diaphragm, whereas a whisper would have been more intelligible. When a man, in ascending, dropped his cap into the Hole, our friend shouted a rigmarole, of which the only words we could catch were: " Winter-bottom—coming up the Hole—cut—his head." " Cut his head ? " we enquired sympathetically, and a wrathful shout was the reply. We implored him to spell it, but he was too much offended. Two of us talked to him for ten minutes without getting any clearer, and then somebody upstairs came to the rescue, and explained that the word was " cap," not " cut," and our fear of a sanguinary accident was relieved. The little comedy was, I hear, much appreciated in the gallery.

Meanwhile the arrivals at the lower terminus were proceeding into the cavern and fixing candles in the natural sconces furnished by the encrusted walls, to prepare for a grand illumination. This did not, however, surpass our previous flare-up, and I need not describe their doings in detail. It was dark before the last half-dozen men could begin their ascent, and the difficulties caused by the twisting together of the ropes became very serious. One or two men received hard knocks in the dark. Coming up with a fish-wife's basket full of lamps, batteries, and other paraphernalia on one arm, whilst in the other hand I carried up a stake, I experienced a sudden stoppage some sixty feet from the top; the main-rope, the life-line, and the telephone wire had got entangled with the rocks. Thus encumbered, I had to be lowered and drag myself along the cliff for several feet in the dark to undo the tangle; then letting go, I shot sideways through the blackness in a thrilling dive. At this juncture the telephone wire broke, and, as the life-line had become a positive danger, we resolved to dispense with it. The handy man in charge on the far side inspected the trolley anxiously from time to time, and, pouring oil on the wheel, tried to stop its disconcerting scream. The wind blew shrill, and it was impossible to keep a candle alight, but here and there electric lamps shone over the toiling band, and penetrated a little way into the darksome jaws of the pit; it was a weird and memorable scene. And now but one man remained in the depths. A whistle announced that he was ready, and the apparatus began to creak for the last time. He came up singing and waving a lighted candle in either hand, happy as a successful explorer deserves to be, and as he came within the glare of our lamps a hearty cheer went up from every one of the throng.

So ended a day that Peak Forest will long remember, longer perhaps than the friends of those who took part in it, and who stand a chance in future ages of figuring in some vague legend of the Victorian era. But it is reported, there are people in the locality still too sceptical, or, shall I say, too credulous, to admit that we really got to the bottom of Elden Hole.

K

XXII.

IN THE SPEEDWELL CAVERN.

EXPLORING THE " BOTTOMLESS PIT."

ELDEN HOLE is only one among many natural pits, chambers, and galleries, that exist in the limestone regions of Derbyshire and the West Riding. Not far away the Blue John Mine leads into a maze of passages and caverns, brilliantly adorned with fluor-spar, calcite crystals, and stalactites; and near it is Peak Cavern, with its long series of vaults and lofty halls, watery tunnels, and mysterious swallows. All these, it has been conjectured, have connections with each other, and with the Speedwell. However that may be, the ramifying Bagshawe Cavern is quite distinct from their system, though not many miles away; and so are the caves near Eyam and Stoney Middleton, the Merlin Cave, and Carl's Wark or Charleswork. Of all the caverns that pierce these hills only an insignificant portion have been or ever will be discovered by man; so at least one may conclude from the story of the Speedwell Cavern.

A lead-mining company in the eighteenth century, driving a shaft into the hillside between the Winnats and Peak Cavern, came across a series of natural chambers, and ultimately broke into an extraordinary cavity, of depth and height unknown, at a point some 650 feet below the surface. Such was the discovery of the famous Speedwell Cavern. The shaft they drove is now blocked up, but people in Castleton know its situation, and their tunnels, with the natural chambers connected therewith can be traced for a mile or more beyond the great cavern.   The miners were much troubled by springs, and apparently to get rid of the water in some way, they cut a level for 750 yards from the present entrance into the mine, to reach the great cavern on the other side.   The company spent a fortune on their excavations, and used 50,000 pounds of blasting powder, without getting any reward for eleven years of work.   They were ruined, and the only result of their enterprise was to leave the tunnel, the cave, and the so-called " Bottomless Pit " accessible to summer crowds of gaping and shuddering tourists.

The Speedwell Cavern was formed by the dissolving and washing away of a part of the great vein known as the New Rake, and runs (see diagram) at a steep angle through the limestone, like a huge tunnel.   In past ages, probably, it was the channel of a subterranean river.   When the miners broke into this hollow they built a causeway across the abyss, and, driving their levels on for a great distance, they excavated 40,000 tons of rock, so it is reported, which they flung into the void.   It is also asserted that these masses of débris did not appreciably raise the level of the water in the supposed unfathomable pool at the bottom, and this dark, mysterious gulf was at once enrolled among the Wonders of the Peak.   Until a comparatively recent date the character and extent of the " Bottomless Pit " were almost entirely unknown, and the visitor to this " terrific void," as the guide-book of 1837 terms it, " vast as Milton's palace of Pandemonium, and filled with impenetrable darkness," was stirred to a high pitch of awe and enthusiasm by conjectures of mighty vaults and unsounded abysses under his feet, where the torrent and the débris found a channel into the bowels of the earth. "The nerves of that man must be firm and well-strung," says Rhodes in his "Peak Scenery" (1824), "who in this situation can contemplate the space around him without shuddering. Standing in the midst of a gulph, where all below is dark vacuity of immeasurable depth, above a mighty cavern whose loftiest recesses no light can reach, and all around uncertain and obscure, an awful feeling takes possession of every faculty, and breath and thought and motion are nearly suspended." The explorers of Elden Hole were allured by these apparently far superior attractions to undertake a thorough investigation of the "Bottomless Pit," and attempt to solve the mysteries connected with it.

Lowering tackle and other apparatus having previously been rigged up inside the cavern, we assembled on May 4th, 1901, at the Peak Hotel in Castleton, and at 6-30 p.m. set out for the Speedwell amidst a crowd of spectators. A cottage of quite ordinary appearance affords entrance to the vaulted flight of a hundred steps leading down to the tunnel, which was turned into an underground canal by the irruption of water into the workings. Hard by are the crags of the Winnats, a rocky defile resembling Cheddar Cliffs in Somerset, just as the neighbouring caverns in the mountain limestone resemble the wonderful caves of Cheddar. The inevitable photograph taken of the two dozen explorers in their panoply, we went downstairs to the boats in two parties. This subterranean voyage is always impressive. Our boatman bids us keep heads and hands well inside, for fear of contact with the rugged walls and roof; and, sticking candles here and there in sockets fixed for that purpose, he shows how straight is the long lane of water lit by these twinkling stars. When we thought of the vast weight of superincumbent

rock, and of the hapless miners who toiled eleven years
fruitlessly in this rat-hole, amid perils from water and
perils from falling rocks, the weirdness of the grim
waterway was intensified. Our own adventure was as
yet a doubtful one as to the issue, and when the dull
booming of the distant waterfall, plunging in full force

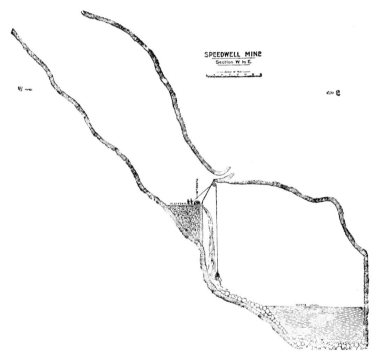

SECTIONAL DIAGRAM OF THE "BOTTOMLESS PIT," SPEEDWELL MINE.

By H. Arnold Bemrose, M.A., F.G.S.

into the " Bottomless Pit," waxed as we came near to
a deafening roar, we almost began to experience some
of the sensations recorded by the grandiloquent Rhodes.

On the platform of the causeway, piles of rope, planks,
photographic apparatus, cylinders of gas, and a huge
quantity of miscellaneous implements lying about,

showed that our friends had made great preparations against our coming. At the edge of the chasm, where a stout iron railing protects the visitor, the tackle for the descent had been erected. A scaffold-pole was fixed across to a crevice in the roof to carry the pulley, and a ladder rested beside it for convenience in working and examining the apparatus. Over the pulley ran ninety yards of Alpine Club rope carrying a wooden seat; a life-line was attached to this, and later on a guy-rope was tied underneath and worked from the rocky slope below, whilst a fourth rope was used for sending down timber and various appliances. A new and extremely powerful illuminant had been devised by the photographer, Mr. Harry Bamforth, of Holmfirth, and the cavern, with its black pit and the strange roof piercing the hill for hundreds of feet overhead, was lit up by such a glare of light as had never shone there before. But when the search-light was projected into the mysterious depths, it only revealed the water foaming over black rocks down to an inky pool, whose shape and farther recesses were lost in gloom. This waterfall can be shut off to a considerable extent by means of a hatch regulating the flow in the canal, and this was now done. Everything was in readiness, and the moment had arrived for the leading man to be hoisted over the railings into the swing chair and make the descent. With an electric lamp tied on in front, he swung over the darkness, and then was let down slowly. It was soon apparent that he would be drenched by the waterfall, diminished as it was; but at that instant he signalled to be drawn up again. Then, armed with a pole, he guided himself down, and at a depth of 40 feet, but many feet away horizontally, he came to a standstill, whether at the bottom or on the brink of another fissure we could not discern. All around was blackness. He

signalled all safe, and attached the guy-rope, and thereupon Mr. Bamforth descended, and some of the
illuminating and photographic apparatus was lowered,
while the two geologists of the party, Mr. H. Arnold
Bemrose, F.G.S., and Dr. Lyster Jameson, followed
and began their important researches at once. I went
down next, bringing more apparatus; and now the
search-light shone out, and the actual character of the
" Bottomless Pit " was disclosed. We were standing
on a sharp slope of broken rocks at the foot of the cliff,
over which the water discharges, and finds its way to
a pool forty feet beyond us. This pool, as we afterwards found by measurement, is twenty-seven yards
long and fourteen wide. Overhead was an arching roof
about fifty feet high, with a slanting funnel in it that
appeared to extend higher. The walls and the roof of
this large chamber were remarkably smooth and regular;
horizontal lines running all round seemed to indicate
water-levels, but are really lines of bedding. There was
only one fissure opening a passage into the rocks at
the side, and a clean-cut wall of limestone completely
blocked up the cavern at the far end of the pool.

Altogether fifteen men descended, and for some time
I was engaged in working the guy-rope, and striving
to keep each man clear of the water as he was lowered.
Some amount of wetting was unavoidable, and, as a
steady stream ran down the ropes and up my sleeves,
my condition was decidedly moist.

In order to examine the parts of the cavern beyond
the water, it was necessary to construct a raft. A
quantity of planks were let down for this purpose,
several of them sticking fast in the channel of the
cascade, and necessitating a scramble up the watery
rocks to free them. Building the raft was no easy task
on a rocky slope in such a fitful light. Eventually a

rickety species of craft was put together, but it looked so unseaworthy that we signalled for the twenty-foot ladder to be sent down, and, lashing this on underneath, we contrived to steady the affair. With plummet and measuring-line in hand, Mr. Puttrell now embarked, and pushed out on the waters of this sunless pool. When he reported the extreme depth to be twenty-two feet, the last vestige of romance associated with the subterranean lake vanished. He failed to discover any point of exit, or to trace any definite current. Doubtless the waters find an exit deep down; but whether, as M. Martel conjectures, there is any communication with the stream in Peak Cavern is still unascertained.

Meanwhile, Dr. Jameson was employed in fishing the margin of the pool and hunting the walls, in search of specimens of the fauna. He soon had an aquarium of cave-beasts in a ginger-beer bottle, perfectly white creatures—some resembling fine examples of the fresh-water shrimp; some like minute worms and leeches. These animals comprised gnats, earthworms, beetles, "springtails," and various crustaceans, all wanderers from the outside; a blind mite (probably Gamassus), two flat worms (Planaria Alpina and Polycelis Cornuta), an almost colourless "water-flea," with eyes (Gammarus), all thoroughly naturalized in their subterranean habitat; and, most interesting of all, three blind species that have probably been isolated in this dark pool for hundreds of generations—Lipura ambulans, Tomocerus tridentiferus, and Lipura inermis (Tullberg)—L. Wrightii (Carpenter). The last had never hitherto been found in any English cave, but it occurs in the Mitchelstown Cave in Ireland, where Dr. Jameson carried out researches some years since, along with M. Martel, author of " Les Abîmes," and the most indefatigable explorer of caves that has ever lived.

Photo by   H. Banforth.

THE CANAL, SPEEDWELL MINE.

Photo by   H. Bamforth.

THE 'BOTTOMLESS PIT'.

Photo by   *H. Bamforth.*

SPEEDWELL CAVERN, ABOVE THE 'BOTTOMLESS PIT'.

None of the calcareous incrustation that beautifies the inner chamber of Elden Hole was to be found in this cavern. Probably the atmosphere is always too humid for the moisture to evaporate quickly enough, and so deposit the carbonate. I had a striking proof of this high degree of humidity when I explored the small subsidiary cave or gallery already alluded to. Entering with a candle, I was hardly able to see for clouds of vapour; so returning, I left the candle, and took one of the electric lamps instead. Even then my breath made a perceptible haze in this narrow winding passage. I forced myself between the rocks for twenty yards, up the bed of a tributary streamlet, which was lined with soft, tenacious mud. Nowhere was there room to turn round, the place was very wet, and at last I came to a pool, whose surface nearly reached the top of the crevice, and made further progress impossible.

When every feasible investigation had been carried out, and as many photographs secured as could be in an atmosphere now made thick with smoke from our combustibles, we sent up the impedimenta, and returned to the top of the embankment one by one. The return journey was a good deal worse than the descent, for the level of the canal had risen, through the closing of the hatches, and a jet of cold water spurted over each person half-way up, even if he escaped being dragged through the lower part of the cascade. This spectacle, when the magnesium lamps were turned on it, was very agreeable to the onlookers, and so pleased were they on the platform with our sufferings, that they gave us just one taste of the waterfall with the hatch up. Then there was a frantic scurry for shelter that was not to be found, three men being observed struggling to get into the little cavern at the side, whose mouth is only wide enough for one, ere our whistles and shouts of distress softened the hearts of our tormentors, and the hatch was let down again. Everybody was drenched, and most of the candles were extinguished by the flying spray; the roar of the spouting water was tremendous. When my turn came to ascend, a gas-cylinder was given into my charge, and attached to my wrist by a string. Ballasted thus, I was not in a position to defend myself in passing up the waterfall, and my chill baptising was greeted with the usual chorus of laughter. Half an hour earlier an awkward accident had been narrowly averted. Our friends on the causeway had signalled to us to send the ladder up again, and refused point blank to draw up another man till they had it. On examining the main rope, they found several strands worn through by the constant friction of the pulley, and a portion had to be cut away.

Towards 2 a.m. all had returned to the platform in perfect safety, the rite of enclosing the explorers' names in a bottle, to be left in the depths, not being omitted. We had hoped to climb the upward extension of the cavern, which rises into the heart of the hill like a gigantic funnel or gully, at an angle of forty-five degrees. In the bed of it short stakes have been fixed for a considerable distance like rungs of a ladder, and by means of these I went to a height of thirty feet, but there found the bed of the gully broken away, leaving a gap not easy to be traversed. There was no chance of ascending by the methods practised in rock-climbing, for the walls are coated with soft friable deposits; everything was wet and greasy, and destitute of any firm holds. Still, the funnel might be climbed with mechanical aids, and it is stated that the miners actually ascended a long way by a series of wooden steps, until they reached a sheer cliff that arrested them altogether. The height of this funnel—in other words, the total height of the Speedwell Cavern—is estimated to be somewhere between four and five hundred feet. We sent up a fire-balloon with a string attached, but it ignited forty feet up, and two rockets hit the sides and rebounded at a height of a hundred feet.

Those men who had not descended into the pit had passed through some laborious and not unexciting hours, for, in hoisting the men and the luggage up and down, they had lifted many foot-tons. Now all were gathered together in the smoky cavern for a final group, one of the most extraordinary photographs, as to conditions and surroundings, ever taken by artificial light. Entering the boats, tired and drenched to the skin, but happy, we returned to the surface of the globe an hour before dawn, and fired a rocket into the moonlight to proclaim our success to the dale of Hope. We were successful, yet disappointed withal, since the terrors of the "Bottomless Pit," notorious far and wide, had proved so far inferior to our hopes and preparations.

XXIII.

THE EXPLORATION OF PEAK CAVERN.

OUR next enterprise, after dispelling the myths associated with the Speedwell Mine, was to explore Peak Cavern, or the Devil's Hole. It resulted in the discovery of a passage between the rocky defile of Cave Dale, behind the castle, and the great cavern known as the "Choir," or the "Orchestra," and of a stalactitic chamber of much beauty, and finally in the re-discovery of certain inner passages and caverns whose very existence had been forgotten for a long period. Curious evidences were found that these passages had at some time or another been worked, or at all events traversed, presumably in search of lead ore.

Preliminary researches were made at intervals during several months by a few members of the Kyndwr Club, and on Saturday, the 1st of March, 1902, the great exploration took place, a large party being engaged in the work. The Sheffield contingent included Messrs. John Cole, M.A., G. F. R. Freeman, Robert McCrum, Percy and John Pearson, J. W. Puttrell, and W. J. Watson; and there came with me from Derby Messrs. R. M. Archer, H. H. Arnold Bemrose, M.A., F.G.S., J. Croft, W. Meakin, W. S. Smith, W. Smithard, and F. Wightman; Mr. H. Bamforth, of Holmfirth, did invaluable work in illuminating the cavern, and Mr. Walker (guide) lent useful assistance. Some twelve of the party made their way considerably further than was achieved by the

French *savant,* M. Martel, who explored Peak Cavern
during the nineties.

Amply equipped with apparatus for rock work,
illumination, and photography, the party left the Peak
Hotel in Castleton about 5 p.m., and ascended Cave
Dale to a corner overlooked by the Peverils' stronghold.
Here an insignificant hole at the cliff's foot gives access
to the newly-discovered passage. At its narrowest the
hole is barely a foot wide, and so low that one has to
crawl on hands and knees. At the end of 21 feet, where
the hole is 2 feet high, an opening 1 foot 2 inches wide
is discerned, leading downwards. This is the new
entrance, and its nature is obviously such as to make it
of little interest to any visitor who is not a speleologist.
Vapour has been observed to rise from the orifice at
certain seasons, indicating a connection with
subterranean waters, and at the bottom remains of
animals show that there is access from above; but the
entrance was partially blocked up with earth and
splinters of rock, which had to be removed before a
man could get in. Mr. Puttrell had, a few days before-
hand, practically demonstrated that perfect communication existed with the lower regions by sending down two
ropes loaded with heavy weights. It was now to be
proved whether a human body could possibly find a way
through.

The explorer was secured from accident by an Alpine
rope 130 feet in length, and a miner's electric lamp was
affixed to his cap, the accumulators being carefully
stowed away to avoid friction. A hauling party
remained above ground, while the majority of us
descended to the cavern by the usual way to see him
arrive, if all went satisfactorily. A crowd of helpers
and spectators were soon assembled in the " Orchestra,"
whence a powerful searchlight was projected into the

lower reaches of the aperture by Mr. Bamforth. We hailed our adventurer. He had already started, and in a few minutes we caught glimpses of his light. The passage is an old watercourse, resembling what climbers would call a gully or a big " chimney," nearly vertical, but in most parts rough enough and narrow enough to allow of back and knee work, or even regular scrambling. Our explorer was actually suspended on the rope only for a brief time. The glimmer of light slowly came nearer, and in thirty minutes after starting Mr. Puttrell reached the bottom, much to the gratification of the many local people who had come to witness this novel exploit.

Hard by the foot of the new passage, in a low-roofed gallery, are a few small stalactites and a good deal of stalagmitic incrustation on the floor. But the Peak Cavern is almost as completely destitute of calcareous deposits of any beauty as the Speedwell Cavern, a circumstance that gives exceptional interest to the discovery of a stalactitic chamber. It is situated near the main entrance, almost in the roof of the main cavern, at a height of sixty feet, where Martel marks down on his chart an aven or shaft. The whole party now adjourned to a spot immediately under the chamber, which had been superficially examined already by some of our friends. A thirty-foot ladder was placed against the cavern wall, and by means of it we reached a roomy recess, to which a second ladder was hauled up and fixed across, almost at right angles, to a second storey. The jagged edge of the stalactite curtain came down close to the second ladder, and one had to wriggle under it in ascending. At the top of the ladder we came to a steep slope of soft tenacious mud, which had to be climbed with care. Everything was dripping with water, the rocks were greasy to the touch, and in manipulating the ropes and ladders, as well as in climbing the rocks, every possible precaution had to be taken against a sudden slip, which might have put the whole of us in jeopardy. The limelight was brought up, and revealed a chamber of some thirty feet by twenty, the walls and dome of which were richly adorned with stalactite in the forms of marble curtains, sculptured reliefs, and pendulous bosses. The floor, too, if it could be called a floor, funnel-shaped, and converging steeply towards the hole up which we had climbed, was covered with similar deposits, where not concealed by mud and clay; and the hard, gritty surface enabled several of us to clamber right round to the highest point, and look up the hole in the roof by the aid of magnesium wire. The hole seemed to dwindle away to nothing; seemingly there was no exit there, and a passage in another corner came to an abrupt end in a yard or two. From the hole overhead a fin-shaped mass of gleaming stalactite curved gracefully downwards for about fifteen feet along the arching roof, a beautiful object. Meanwhile the bottom ladder had been hauled up, and placed across the gap from the slimy floor to a still higher storey, eighty feet from the cave floor. Here, it was hoped, communication would be discovered with another gallery, perhaps with the passages whose exits are visible on the cliff face, right over the main entrance to Peak Cavern. A sloping passage was discovered, lined with the same treacherous mud, its roof hung with small stalactites; but in a few yards it dwindled away, until it was impossible to see anything but a narrow cleft full of thread-like stalactites connecting top and bottom. We left a relic of our visit, in the shape of a new penny to mark the date, and then returned by the way we had come, utilising one of the big stumps of stalagmite on the floor as a belaying-pin in lowering the ladder.

By now it was dark. Looking through the great arched portal to the outer air, one saw only a faint mysterious twilight, yet the grim blackness of the interior, beyond the gleam of the artificial lights, was as impressive as in daytime. The exploring party was now considerably diminished, for the third stage of the work was not of a kind to attract anybody not thoroughly hardened to exposure, and to the possibility of hard knocks. Gathering up the various apparatus and taking one of the ladders, we proceeded through the length of the cavern as far as the " Victoria Hall," hitherto supposed to be the end of the accessible parts. There had been too much rain lately to favour our undertaking. The Devil's Hole Water, we had noticed, was very high, and the streamlets from the cave roof that give a name to " Roger Rain's House " were falling in torrents. Some distance beyond this is a swallow, into which volumes of water were pouring with far-heard rumbling.

Adjacent to the " Victoria Hall," and separated from it by a rocky curtain fifty feet high, is a bell-shaped chamber with a hole at the top. It is supposed that the peculiar resonance of the cavern at this spot is due to the hollow thus existing in its walls. We reached the top of the curtain by means of the ladder, in order to light up the whole of the vast cavern with limelight. Stones dropped through the hole into the bell-shaped chamber made a hollow noise, that re-echoed powerfully through the neighbouring vaults and corridors. On the opposite side of the main cavern a steep slope ascends towards the gigantic upward chasm, whose slightly bell-shaped configuration gave it in olden times the title of Great Tom of Lincoln. The Prussian pastor, C. P. Moritz, who, in 1782, visited Peak Cavern, likens this slope to " a steep hill which was so high that it seemed to lose itself as in a cloud," and the guide's

R.M. Archer. del.

PASSING THROUGH THE SUPPOSED SIPHON IN PEAK CAVERN.

EXPLORING GROTTO IN ROOF OF PEAK CAVERN.

candle at the summit was like " a bright and twinkling
star," an " indescribably beautiful sight." His
description, which, without being untruthful, is
imaginative and even poetical, is one of the best ever
written of Peak Cavern. The scene as we viewed it
was far different, but not less romantic. A powerful
limelight lit up the mysterious cavity overhead, and the
crowd of volunteers and spectators dotted over the
accessible parts revealed the full extent of the floor.

A fire-balloon was sent up. It mounted swiftly till
it came into contact with the walls, it lurched about and
righted itself many times, and then ascended in a slightly
zig-zag fashion, following the trend of the cliff until
it disappeared behind a corner. Rumour has it that the
huge cleft continues up and up until it reaches the surface
of the hill, three hundred feet above. However that may
be, the balloon never saw the sky. A quarter of an
hour later, whilst we were busy with other matters, a
rustling was heard, and the balloon appeared, wafted
slowly down, the methylated spirits burnt out and a
hole in its side. Where had it been ? A rocket was
sent up, but fell again without attaining any great
height, though it looked magnificent; a second rocket
burst prematurely among those who were letting it off.
Right in the angle, where the walls of the chasm come
together, a number of stakes have been fixed by miners
in the old days to form a kind of ladder. Other indications of mining are visible, and a vein of silver and
lead makes a conspicuous mark along one of the walls.

This is the utmost point reached by the ordinary
visitor. About a dozen of us were preparing to go a
good deal further. Our first step was to make our way
through what Martel called a " siphon," a crooked
tunnel nearly full of water, and for this purpose a flat-
bottomed collapsible boat had been provided. The

L

skipper went through first with one passenger; it was unsafe to take more at a time. Both extended themselves flat in the boat, the roof coming so low in parts that even thus it grazed one's nose, and the gunwale grated and jolted against its rugged surface; the boat was propelled by pushing against the sides and roof of the tortuous channel. Beyond the tunnel a bank of sand and gravel intervened in a wider cavern, which we called the " Calcite Cave," on account of the abundance of white translucent pebbles found there; and beyond that again came another channel, also nearly filled with water. I conveyed three or four explorers through the first tunnel, but in my last journey I lost control of the boat in the wider portion, and, stretching over to touch the walls, I fell in. My companion seized my leg and saved me from a complete ducking, but I was extremely glad to send my drenched coat back at the next boat journey. We dragged our skiff over the sandbank and launched it in the second tunnel, Mr. Freeman boldly wading through, although the water came nearly to his chin, and proceeded in the boat to where a projecting rock barred further advance. A stonemason had been employed to cut this away, without effecting much improvement, and there was no help for it but to slip over the gunwale and wade the last few yards through several feet of water and mud. The roof came down close over the boat, and made the manœuvre more awkward. At this point about half of the party undressed and went through the remaining adventures in that condition. The scene reminded one strongly of Mr. Kipling's inimitable extravagance " The Taking of Lungtungpen." They soon covered themselves with a decent coating of mud. I was too well bedrenched already to trouble about removing clothes.

Ahead of us the cavern continued as a long, irregular vault about ten feet high, horizontal or gently rising, with streams and pools here and there, their beds paved with calcite pebbles. Even with a powerful light it is quite difficult to see still water in a cavern. You see before you a shallow or a deep trough or basin paved with sand and pebbles, every spot and wrinkle of which is perfectly clear; and if you are not too well acquainted with this kind of trap, in you plunge, up to the knees in ice-cold water. The pure unrippled water is often practically invisible, even at the short distance of a foot or two, for there is no sunlight to turn the surface into a shining mirror. Several of the party were ensnared in this manner. The limestone walls and roof were black with a uniform coating of thick adhesive mud. In this place, which is a long way beyond the limits of Martel's investigations, a curious discovery was made— by Mr. M'Crum, I believe. A wooden sled measuring two and a half feet by one foot, waterlogged and full of mud, lay at the stream side. It had rounded iron runners, and was probably used for carrying ore. The interesting relic was conveyed to the vestibule of the cavern, where, I trust, it will be carefully preserved. Who shall tell us its date or its history? At all events it is irrefragable testimony to a human occupation of this innermost section of the cavern, and a considerable distance further we found other indications of work by miners which, though I was sceptical at first, I am bound to say have convinced me. We had come at length to what appeared to be the end of everything, and Mr. Freeman, who was in front, called out " Cul-de-sac! " We were about to turn back when he saw a hole between the wall and the floor, hardly bigger than a rabbit-hole, and began scraping away with his hands. He pushed a candle in, then his head; his shoulders stooped through the hole, and in another moment he had disappeared. I followed as best I might, and found a slough of mud and water just inside, which had to be waded through on hands and knees. We got perhaps fifty feet further, and then stopped indeed at the bottom of a natural fissure that rose to a height of twenty feet or so. But what interested us most was a bank of stones, apparently built up in regular courses, showing, beyond a doubt, that at some period, near or remote, this part of the cavern was searched by miners.

Whilst we were in this narrow inner chamber a somewhat startling incident occurred. A shout was heard feebly through the narrow hole to the effect that the water was rising. We immediately hurried back the way we had come, and learned that it was a false alarm. There had been a sudden flow from an intermittent spring in a branching gallery, which, coming when all was silence, had been very puzzling and disquieting. We found that the water was running into a large swallow, into the upper part of which I descended about eight feet, and looked into the formidable pit beneath. We could see nothing through the falling water, but a boulder flung in raised the booming sound that means deep water. We flung in another and another; the noise was awful in such a place; the echoes ran in appalling drum-beats along the vaults and died away in the further passages. Undaunted by this, Mr. Freeman offered to be let down by a rope, and actually descended to the water, thirty feet down, right through the cascade, which, of course, put his light out. There was nothing to indicate its depth.

While the rest of the party were removing their muddy disguise and dressing themselves, three of us thought we would take time by the forelock and be off to the hotel. Two launched the boat on the waters of the

Photo by   H. Bamforth.

PEAK CAVERN – THE FIVE ARCHES.

outer tunnel, and the third, who had nothing on but
his boots, obligingly pushed us through. He seemed
to be a little absent-minded in dressing. First he lost
his socks, and in the excitement of not finding them he
somehow forgot to put on his shirt—at least, we
supposed that was the reason, for he walked home with
the shirt over his arm, and looked a striking object in
the unearthly gloom. We met with unexpected
obstacles in trying to make our exit from the cavern.
In the " Victoria Hall " the smoke of our lights and
fireworks would probably hang about for a week; at
present it made a dense fog that our one sound candle
failed entirely to illumine. We could not see a pace
and a half before our noses, and all the candles that
had been stuck here and there as guide-posts had long
ago burned out. On every side the noise of water,
running and tumbling, was heard, confounding our
sense of direction, and by no means helping us to avoid
a wetting. One man stepped into the brook before we
had any idea we were near it. Anxious to make ourselves useful, we were taking a ladder out to the cave-
mouth; but we had only just congratulated ourselves
on getting so well ahead of the dawdlers when we came
to a full-stop. The cavern we were following was not
the main cavern at all, and we recognised a dead end,
where, in a branching tunnel, a shower of water drizzles
incessantly from a cleft in the roof hard by a siphon.
Back we went, carefully exploring every foot of the way
with our precious candle, which we guarded anxiously,
lest a drip from the roof should put it out and leave us
to shiver in the dark until the others caught us up.
Now we struck into a well-trod path and hurried onward;
anon, to our astonishment, we came upon water again,
and, to our disgust, there was our battered ferry-boat—
we had actually returned to our starting point.

Eventually we did hit upon the right track, and, once clear of the blinding fumes, made our way swiftly through the echoing arcades out to the open air.

The other men came out shortly after, nothing of any importance being done after midnight. Whether, after these investigations, any further discoveries of an important kind will ever be made here one cannot say; the limestone teems with possibilities, but it is hardly to be expected unless engineering methods are adopted. I have searched the oldest histories and topographical accounts of Derbyshire in vain for any reference to lead-mining in Peak Cavern; it is impossible to say how many centuries may have elapsed since the owner of the mysterious sled risked his life in these unknown caves. Perhaps he kept the secret of their existence to himself and let it die with him; at all events, their history has been totally forgotten.

XXIV.

THE BLUE JOHN MINE.

A FTER their autopsy of the Devil's Hole or Peak Cavern, our explorers proceeded to turn the Blue John Mine and all its ramifying passages inside out. For some considerable time several members of the Kyndwr Club, Mr. J. Royse, the lessee of the mine, co-operating, carried out minute and exhaustive investigations, and on Saturday, April 26th, 1902, a regular field-day was organised (if such a phrase can be used for operations that lasted nearly all night), a narrative of which will give a good idea of the results attained. The exploring party numbered fully two dozen, all of whom were members and friends of the Kyndwr Club. The Rev. D. Macdonald (president) and the secretary, Mr. F. Wightman, were among the workers, and Messrs. R. M. Archer, Harold Brodrick, W. O. Dobson, R. McCrum, and W. Meakin took a leading part. Of the discoveries made the most interesting was a great shaft or aven beautifully incrusted with huge masses of stalactite; certain connecting galleries unknown to Messrs. Barnes and Holroyd, who explored the cave very thoroughly in the years 1893-6, but apparently suspected to exist by M. Martel, who made a cursory survey in 1895, were fully worked out; while a series of important caves, overlooked altogether by the above-named explorers but visited in 1857 by Mr.

B. Tym, were carefully examined, and materials
thus acquired for a full and connected knowledge of
this interesting mine with its intricate series of caves.

The party of explorers entered the mine about 6-30
p.m. I need not repeat the descriptions so often given
of the caves ordinarily seen by the public; I shall therefore pass over the Ladies' Walk, the Grand Crystallised
Cavern, etc., and take up the thread where we turned
out of the Stalactite Cavern, which precedes the well-
known Lord Mulgrave's Dining-room, and descended
by a steep and tortuous staircase, cut artificially, into
a low passage that led eventually into what Messrs.
Barnes and Holroyd call the " New Cavern," but which
is locally designated the " Stemple Cavern," on account
of the ladder of stakes leading out at the far end. In
many places already we had been forced by the narrow-
ness of the passages to go in a stooping posture, and
even on hands and knees. Encumbered with cameras,
ropes, ladders, gas cylinders, limelight, and the numberless articles necessary in a thorough exploration, we
made no very rapid progress over this difficult ground.
The air seemed quite warm and close after the fresh
breezes on the hill outside. This New Cavern, which
is a hundred yards long, is well worth visiting, for
many reasons. It is floored unevenly with rough blocks,
under which a small stream gurgles; the steeper part
is rather an awkward place to traverse in a bad light.
Here and there on the straight and lofty walls are frozen
cascades, so to speak, of snowy stalactite; for, unlike
the other local caves, the Blue John series abounds with
the most beautiful deposits, of all colours and varieties
of form, from the purest and most translucent calcareous
matter to the deep violet of the fluor spar. Here also
are some of the largest masses of coral and encrinites,
the limestone walls frequently exhibiting the beautiful

Photo by   *H. Bamforth.*

THE FAIRY GROTTO – BLUE JOHN MINE.

forms of the " sea-lilies " embossed on the surface, in high relief.

Already we were getting wet. Water drips incessantly in many spots from the roof and ledges, and in the corridor that we now entered we plunged into a perfect slough of mud. The New Cavern points approximately north, and at the end of it a passage turns almost at a right angle down to the Fairy Grotto, a bewitching piece of cave architecture that is by no means flattered by its name. Walls, ceiling, and floor, each fretted into endless shapes and forms, are alike incrusted with gleaming deposits. Across the middle a jammed block makes a sort of bridge; this, too, is covered with the same brilliant enamel, while above it and around there depends from the roof and from the ledges a little forest of thin, thread-like stalactites, many of them two feet in length, and in some places as thickly strung as the chords of a harp. Beyond the Fairy Grotto the passage rapidly dwindles, and presently is almost filled by a stream. M. Martel hints at a theory that there is a connection between this point and a lower and apparently distant series of galleries by way of a steep tunnel, which, he says, he would not venture to climb without a companion (see " Mémoires de la Société de Spéléologie," tome iv., No. 23, July, 1900). The instinct of the great speleologist was not at fault, for it was presently demonstrated that two persons could see and shake hands with each other from points that, in walking distance, were three-quarters of a mile apart, though the rock above came too close to the rocky floor to permit one to wriggle through. I was strongly advised by our leader to undress and try to make a passage, and might perhaps have succeeded in that condition, but it was at the end of a long and tiring seven hours of work, and I declined the honour.

But to return to the right-angled elbow, already mentioned, between the New Cavern and the Fairy Grotto—someone had discovered a fine shaft or fissure at some distance above the ground, and it was now proposed to send a party of rock-climbers up to explore. Now began the most exciting incidents of the whole exploration, the interest being all the keener because the discoveries were perfectly new. Two ladders bound together were raised almost vertically to the lowest ledge of the rocks above us, for the shaft was virtually the upper parts of a gigantic fissure, of which the lower parts were the accessible passages of the cave. Mr. Puttrell mounted the rocks, and in a few more feet found himself on the lower part of a kind of cascade of stalagmite, the tail of the vast curtain of calcite that lined the walls of the fissure as far up as we could see. Mr. Watson followed Puttrell; I came next, and was followed by Mr. Brodrick, one hundred and thirty feet of rope being used to connect the four. We climbed with candles in our hands, lumps of clay making the most effective candlesticks, and proving peculiarly useful for sticking the light on the wall whilst we hunted about for handhold and foothold. Puttrell climbed ahead up the " chimney " in front, chiefly by means of back and knee work, the smooth surface of the stalagmite crust offering few grips, whilst the wet made one's hands slip alarmingly. While he advanced steadily, backed up by Watson, the other two of us, with a long interval of rope, stationed ourselves on the base of the cascade of stalagmite and hauled up two planks, which we fixed across the opening underneath us, and so constructed a flimsy platform for Mr. Bamforth to place his camera upon. More men now came up, and we at once followed the two climbers. They reached a height estimated at one hundred and

thirty feet above the cave floor, and thought it prudent
to go no further. High above our heads the rays of the
electric lamps and the magnesium lit up the snow-white
reaches of the shaft and beamed through pure,
translucent folds and globes of stalactite and stalagmite.
Some of the pipe-shaped deposits were crystallised, and
reflected the light from a thousand facets. The highest
point I reached was about a hundred feet up, where I
stood on a rock that bridged the gulf. Upwards I saw
right into the curved and twisted rift, a vision of wild
beauty, and downwards I looked on a scene that was
amusing in spite of the eeriness of our situation. On
the two planks, eighty feet below, a full-plate camera
was erected, and looked ready to topple over on the
heads of the men holding lights at the bottom of the
cave. The photographer dexterously got the focus and
snatched his view without going behind the camera, and
now proceeded to the delicate task of getting the instrument down. All the while bits of rock were falling on
everybody from the climbers overhead, the various ropes
were getting entangled in the fitful light, and the curious
echoes of the place added to the seeming confusion.
Everything, however, was conducted slowly and in
order; the ropes were straightened out, and now the
climbing party began to return. This was far more
ticklish than the ascent had been, especially for the
last man down, and we were glad when it was safely
accomplished. The new shaft is certainly one of the
finest things to be seen in any British cave, and it is
a pity that it should be so inaccessible. A few months
later four of the party came again and climbed it
practically to the top, which was not so much farther up
as we thought.

About 11 p.m. all had assembled in the great Dining-
room, and, in spite of clay and candle-grease, were

enjoying the sandwiches just sent up from the hotel. For picturesque weirdness the scene in this huge natural hall rivalled any painting of caverns and bandits that Salvator Rosa ever imagined. The hall is a vast irregular dome, where the several passages of the Blue John Cavern meet, as the limbs of a cathedral meet under the lantern. Massive ribs spring from the clean-cut walls, and form great craggy pendants on the roof, with shadowy hollows between them. We were a motley and savage-looking crowd, lolling about on the cave-floor, with our miscellaneous ideas as to the proper attire for pot-holing, the variety, howbeit, toned down by the general coating of mud. Faces and hands, too, were as grimy as our clothes. As the moving shafts of the limelight glanced over us and the magnesium powder leapt up in intolerable sheets of light, the spectacle was almost infernal, what with the black super-human shadows and the lurid glare shifting over walls and roof of our strange chamber. But we were quickly on the move again, and once more quitted the caves that are shown to the public. From the railings, a little way further, the visitor is allowed to look into the shadowy recesses of the Variegated Cavern, a lofty vault distinguished by the massive and almost columnar structure of its walls and roof, where the angle of the beds and joints of the limestone forming Tray Cliff, part of a steep anticline, is plainly exhibited. Here and in the Crystallised Cavern those curious growths of fungi covered with a concretion of carbonate make dark patches like fur upon the walls, which glitter with dog-tooth crystals in contrast. A stream runs down the rugged staircase of blocks, many of them as large as those in the roof, and is lost to sight in the blackness beyond. We follow, and at the bottom of the slope come to a swallow, near the spot where Martel's Galérie

Inférieure " ascends to the left and ultimately reaches
the Fairy Grotto.   We found this gallery not very
difficult to climb.   Here and there were openings in the
walls and shafts in the roof that looked promising, but
did not allure us; the Blue John Mine is almost
inexhaustible, with its winding network of shafts and
corridors.   Our attention was mainly turned to the
series of chambers that lie beyond the limit of Barnes
and Holroyd's explorations.   At the head of a slope
above the swallow we came to a steep bank of clay,
practically blocking up a great arch that beckoned to
things beyond.   The party divided, some escalading
the bank, and the rest of us, one by one, creeping into
a sort of big rabbit-hole in the bottom part of this
rampart.   We found ourselves, indeed, in something
very much like a rabbit's burrow.   Stretched at full
length, we crawled on our stomachs, candle in hand,
until we came to a hole suddenly opening downwards,
into which we let ourselves glide gently, and by means
of thrusting knees and elbows against the clay-lined
walls descended about forty feet into a lower cave where
a stream ran.   On our left a curtain of rock arose steeply
to a knife-edge.   This we climbed with much difficulty,
and two of us found ourselves sitting astride the knife-
edge with an abyss on the further side.   The leading
man was now roped to go down the steeper side of
the curtain.   At a depth of thirty feet he landed on a
floor of rock and clay, and when I had been lowered
also, we found we were in the bottom of a lofty and
grandly proportioned cavern, with the precipitous
curtain behind us, a gigantic mass of stalactite draping
a rift that extended from floor to ceiling in front, and
far up above, in a sort of balcony at the side, and cut
off from us by a craggy gap, were the lights of
the party who had separated from us half an hour

ago. The initials of Mr. B. Tym on the wall, roughly written with a stone on the blackened limestone, recorded a visit made in 1857; the cavern seems not to have been found again till 1897, when Mr. Royse penetrated as far.

One of the scramblers ascended some distance into the rift in front, walking on tiers of incrusted ledges that looked most wonderful as the electric lamp stole about among their seldom-illumined traceries. Some of the wavy masses, with a lamp shining behind or in front, exhibited the ruddy tinge due to oxide of iron, though as a rule the deposits of carbonate here are exquisite in their virgin whiteness. With a friend I proceeded meanwhile into a watery tunnel at the side. For nearly twenty yards we followed a stream that flowed over black, yielding mud, in which we waded knee-deep; then we could get no further. Even here the omnipresent deposits made glittering veins on roof and walls. A number of the party insisted on coming to the furthest point attained in our exploration, and the difficulty of putting each man over the curtain and letting him down the sheer and ledgeless side caused much delay, though the job of getting them back was twice as hard. The bottom of the big cavern was found to be forty by nineteen feet in area; but it broadens as it rises; and indeed this might be considered as only one compartment of the bottom, the chamber on the nearer side of the curtain being spanned by the same vast roof. The height could not be much less than a hundred feet. We sent up a lighted balloon, which revealed the grandeur of the broad, capacious roof and lit up the group of our friends in the lofty gallery. When, after a severe struggle in getting back over the curtain and up the rabbit-hole, I returned to the main passage, I climbed the bank to this gallery and looked over the edge, perilously edged with huge fallen blocks, on to the workers in the pit below. Some interesting photographs were obtained in this strange spot, which reminds one somewhat of the " Orchestra " in Peak Cavern. Other passages than the rabbit-hole, but more dangerous and difficult, were found to communicate with the final series of caves.

Looking at the charts sketched by previous explorers, I see that the various caves and passages can now be connected into a fairly complete system—so far, that is, as concerns the more important chambers. Plenty, of course, always remains for explorers with better appliances or more determination, but these latest researches have done a little to simplify the bewildering maze of streamlets and tunnels. From the point of view of a seeker of the picturesque these less-known parts of the Blue John Cavern are abundantly attractive. In one sense the Blue John Mine is dry, though the condition of one's clothes would seem to give the lie to such a statement. Dr. Jameson, moreover, was unable to find much evidence of animal life, and thought the excessive humidity of the cavern was the reason of this. Nevertheless the cavern is devoid of any such streams as fill one's ear in Peak Cavern with the roar of invisible waters, and there are hardly any of those grim, mysterious swallows that are so sensational to hear and to see. But the main expansions of the tunnels are all exceedingly grand and majestic in structure, and the range of minerals forming beautiful deposits is almost unique. In the Cheddar Caves alone have I seen anything to compare with these, and even at Cheddar there is nothing to compare with the deep violet bands of delicate veins of the Blue John when its beauties can be seen. The exploration party returned to the surface just before 2 a.m. A keen wind was blowing, and the sudden change of temperature almost made us loth to come out of doors. And the change of scenery, from the grandeur of the natural vaults and the weirdness of the black shadows and the artificial lights, to the frosty glimmer of the moon across the zenith and the long, dark, jagged line of the ridge from Lose Hill to Mam Tor's bald top, emerging out of the sea of shadows in Hope Vale, was like passing into another world.

XXV.

EXPLORING THE BAGSHAWE CAVERN
AT BRADWELL.

O F the caverns in the neighbourhood of Castleton, the least known to tourists is the one at Bradwell, called the Bagshawe Cavern. It is much bepraised by some of the guide-books, which allot two hours as the minimum time for inspecting it; yet the parts accessible to the public form but a small proportion of the whole, and for long it has been supposed that its ramifications extend several miles, and that wonderful sights await the explorer in its inmost recesses. Since the latter part of 1901 a number of interesting discoveries have been made beyond the points previously attained, some adventurous villagers being among the explorers. On Saturday, June 14th, 1902, with three companions, Messrs. P. and F. Pearson, and W. Smithard, I went over the whole of the ground recently discovered, and we succeeded in making our way along certain passages which appear never to have been visited hitherto. Arrangements had been made for an exploration by a much larger party, but it was predicted by persons whose local knowledge made their opinion formidable that the main passages would be filled by the recent rains. This, however, turned out to be a mistake, such floods occurring only in times of very heavy rainfall, and usually in winter. The four explorers entered the cavern at 5-45 p.m. Descending the long flight of steep and narrow steps, we passed through the Fairies'

M

Kitchen and the Bellhouse, and by the entrance to the Straits of Gibraltar and Calypso's Cave, without wasting any time in looking at these celebrated attractions, and made a halt at the Dungeon, the utmost point reached by the ordinary visitor. We deposited our ropes, ladder, hurricane lamps, and the reserve stock of illuminants here, for we proposed making this our starting-point for two journeys of exploration, one to the east and one to the west. The Dungeon is a grisly-looking chasm about twenty feet deep, which forms a most important link in the chain of caverns, since it is the connecting shaft between the upper and the lower series of passages, and in flood-time carries the overflow from the one to the other. At such times the Dungeon fills with water, and apparently the next section of the cavern, which rises for some distance before it begins to fall, is converted by means of this column of water into a siphon that discharges into the new, or lower, series of caves. The guide had a theory, of which more presently, that the water eventually finds its way thus to a large chamber and passage recently explored for some distance from Bradwell Dale. It will be well for the reader to grasp a general idea of the lie of the main passages, in order to understand the scope of our explorations. From the Dungeon we have this new series of caves, the lower, running in an easterly direction; then roughly parallel is the unexplored tunnel through which the Bradwell river flows; whilst by following the upper series of caves from the Dungeon in the other direction, we shall meet the Bradwell river again at a much higher point of its course. No doubt, each set of caves represents a former channel of the river, which has forsaken them one by one as it worked its way to a lower line of fissures in the manner common to the water-systems of limestone regions. The lower series of caves were discovered last year. M. Martel, the French speleologist, who devoted little time to the Bagshawe, was unacquainted with them; his chart comes to an end immediately below the Dungeon. Two members of the Kyndwr Club recently explored one main passage to a distance of nearly a mile, and then were stopped by a *cul-de-sac*. We had the satisfaction to-day of proving that other passages exist to right and to left of the one they followed, one at least larger and probably more important as a water-way in times of flood; and we hoped in some abnormally dry season to follow these up and perhaps discover the exit towards Bradwell Dale.

We used a rope ladder for the descent of the Dungeon. Whilst two of us were engaged in sundry preparations, the other two, slenderly provided with candles, went forward with the intention, they said, of examining a curious chamber situated a hundred yards along the main passage. They had not returned in half an hour, so we followed, expecting to join them in a few minutes. We passed through the chamber afore-mentioned, but they were not there, nor were they to be found in a second cave of two storeys a little way beyond, so we decided to push on through the lakelets and the main passages, rather annoyed at their rashness in dividing the party. It is soon necessary to crawl. The passages go up and down, and almost everywhere exhibit marks of a rush of water in winter time. Sandbanks, masses of clay, and beds of gravel indicate where the water was still or violently agitated. Here we went through a tunnel with flattish floor, cut clean and smooth and quite clear of sand and clay; evidently a current must sweep through this place sometimes with great velocity. Then we came to the first water. It was a long pool in the bottom of a low tunnel, and we scrambled clear of it along the margin until we approached the far end, when it was necessary to wade. The next pool was deeper, but by hugging the left wall we avoided going in above our knees. From time to time we shouted to the missing men, but the grim and oppressive silence settled down again; there was no reply.

At every few yards the walls are brightened by incrustations, chiefly in the form of petrified cascades, Now we came to the first of the stalactite chambers, and a very beautiful one it is. So dense are the long, transparent pencils and pendent masses, and so narrow the way, that it was impossible to avoid knocking some of them off, much as we should have wished to save any damage, if only for the sake of our heads. The magnesium ribbon lit up a roof scribbled all over with glittering arabesques, where the carbonate exudes from the cracks. However, we could not delay, our friends were in front, and we had been told by the local wiseacres that a downrush of water was to be expected in this lower channel. We soon reached the third water, a lake about eighty feet long, nearly filling a winding tunnel. In we plunged, making what use we could of the great slabs that lay beneath the surface, though these had a knack of luring one along their flat, firm pavement until one's foot suddenly plunged down into deep water. We groped with our feet, advancing warily, the chill water creeping higher and higher till we were in nearly to our breasts; then the tunnel makes an abrupt turn and the lake shallows. Little did we think as we struggled out, dripping wet, that we were destined to go through this ordeal four times before the day's work, or rather the night's work, was finished.

More creeping and crawling, more climbing over rugged piles of limestone blocks mixed up with black masses of toadstone, which abounds here to a remarkable degree, and we arrived at the second stalactite chamber, much the finest of any yet discovered in this series of caves. Though it lacks the natural bridge that adds such a weird touch of beauty to the Fairy Grotto in the Blue John Mine, this is even richer in stalactites. When the magnesium flashed out it lit up a long perspective of pendulous wands, some white, some deeply tinged with red and saffron, many of them crystal-clear, like a frozen shower. Some were shaped like curving folds of drapery, and were stained with colour bands by the various deposits in the calcite. Struck with a piece of stone they gave out musical notes. Afterwards, on coming back to this spot, I wriggled down into a hole under the floor, and found a pool of clear water covered with a crust of carbonate as thin as paper.

On we went again, now walking upright through high-roofed corridors, now going on hands and knees over sharp boulders that cut our legs severely, and now wriggling under low rocks on our breasts. Oftentimes the chambers, though low, were as much as thirty feet wide, and the place reminded one of a coal-mine where the men are working in cramped positions at a very shallow seam. Still we had not overtaken our friends, and still there was no answer to our shouting. All of a sudden we heard noises like the fall of big stones in the distance or the sound of someone hammering loudly on the rocks. We could not tell whence the sound proceeded, but it seemed to come from overhead. Presently we saw a round object in the middle of the floor; it was an apple; our friends had evidently gone this way and left it for a landmark. Unfortunately the cave now began to ramify, and the more important passage was not always the more obvious. We began to feel anxious when we came to a big chamber whence the only apparent exit was down a wide, low-arched opening, floored with sand and pebbles, and evidently the dry bed of a considerable stream. I crawled down this for a little distance, and saw that it was a practicable way for some distance further; but the bed showed no sign that any one had ever traversed it, at all events since the last flood. It would have been impossible to crawl through without leaving marks, so we returned at once, for it was not safe to attempt to explore a long passage until the party was re-united.

Had the others returned also and passed us in our wanderings? Whatever had occurred, we must get back to the main passage before taking any further steps. To do this seemed a simple undertaking, but we had gone perhaps two furlongs in a backward direction when it struck one of us that we had never seen this place before. We had not only quitted the main passage, but also lost all idea of its whereabouts. It is in such a situation that one has some sympathy with the solitary explorer suddenly smitten with cave fright. More by luck than skill we managed to regain the old route after a quarter of an hour's wandering, and eventually we got back to the apple, which remained just as it was. Of course there was just a chance that our friends had returned and left it. Otherwise, even had no accident befallen them, they were in an awkward plight, for their candles had most likely burnt away before this. We were, however, quite unprepared for a protracted search, and we resolved that it was safest to return forthwith to the top of the Dungeon, ascertain whether our comrades had got back, and if not start fully prepared to discover them. Back we went through all those low tunnels and cold pools again, and at the end of what seemed a long journey reached the Dungeon. Our friends had not returned.

We ate a sandwich and drank some water. Then, whilst my companion got together some twine, a reel of silk, and a hundred foot rope to mark out our trail, and packed the waterproof box with candles, I re-ascended to the entrance to see if a fifth man, whom we half expected, had arrived on the scene. He had not come, so I filled my pockets with candle-ends and returned, whereupon our search party of two set out on the second journey into the new caves. Before starting we anxiously discussed whether it would not be advisable to secure help from friends in the village. The fall of rocks that we had heard a long while before made us apprehend an accident; then, again, we knew that the branching passages were very extensive, and the task before us might be a formidable one. Being loath, however, to make unnecessary stir, we decided to do our own best first, at all events. For the third time we went back through the long succession of pools and tunnels, and at length we again reached that important geographical point, the apple. Both the apple and our marks round it were still untouched, and still as we hurried forward our hails were unanswered. We passed one of the diverging passages and were approaching the point where we had gone astray, when, to our delight, a shout came feebly from somewhere in front, and in a few minutes we found the absentees sitting round a fast-expiring candle, the only bit they had left.

It appeared that they first of all followed the passage discovered recently, and traced it right to its termination near a large swallow. Returning, as they thought, into the main cavern, they had gone astray in a new passage, which they followed up for half a mile, crawling for a large part of the way over a stony river bed. They had not reached the end of this passage, which grew into a wide and lofty tunnel further on, and will no doubt be worth tracing to its end under more favourable conditions. Once more they made a desperate attempt to regain the main route, and then the supply of candles failed, and when we found them they had resigned themselves to the prospect of waiting for help. In fact, they were quite prepared to spend the night there. We scolded them politely, but felt that their rashness had been fully expiated by their subsequent experiences. Anyhow, they had found a new and important series of passages, whilst we had discovered another series, and this was well worth the toil and tribulation. Somewhere in the course of their wanderings they had come across a candle, still alight, which we had left behind, but this was not sufficient by itself to indicate the road to the Dungeon. And a more curious thing was that they, too, had heard the noise of rocks falling which had struck us with such misgivings. Whether these were natural noises, caused by water, or what they were, we could not make out.

Again we set out on the long and tedious obstacle race to the Dungeon, now become painfully familiar. There was no hurry this time, and we examined the stalactite chambers at leisure. By 11 p.m. we had returned to the head of the Dungeon, had some refreshment, and were ready to start on our next venture, into the upper series of caves. These passages are as rugged and constricted as the lower ones, and are less interesting, lacking the wealth of stalactitic deposits. In about half a mile a hollow murmur breaks on the ear, the far-away rumble of a torrent. As we approached, the murmur waxed to a deafening roar; it sounded like the noise of a high waterfall or a very big swallow. Now we came to the branch whence the noise proceeded, and following it down for a few yards we found the Bradwell river bubbling up from the sides and rushing

tumultuously away into the thick darkness of a tunnel.
After our fatigues we were in no fit state to follow the
river any distance, so we returned to the point of
divergence and made our way along the main passage
again, where we could discern another noise of waters,
evidently caused by the same stream higher up. The
sixty-feet waterfall that the guide-books talk about is
purely mythical; doubtless the mysterious sound of this
water has caused the mistake. The guide to the cavern,
who is also a poet, tells very amusingly what happened
when the first explorers reached this spot :—

> Now here the waters they did rage!
> It put them in a fright,
> So that one man, although a sage,
> Ran back with all his might.

The last hundred yards were as bad as any we had
tackled. The fissure was low and flat—so low that we
had to lie on our sides and wriggle, unable even to raise
our heads. Then at last our candles shone across a
broad sheet of water coming swiftly towards us and disappearing under the stones over which we were crawling.
The Pearsons had got three hundred feet higher last
week, but we were stopped here by the increase of the
water. Whether anybody will ever succeed in getting
far beyond this point in a season of drought is very
doubtful indeed, for there appears to be a siphon there.
The river tunnel, on the other hand, may be worth
exploring further. We had now carried out our plan
of investigation, and were all very tired. One of the
two who had been lost became ill at this juncture, and
was too exhausted even to carry his share of
the apparatus. We packed up our goods at the
Dungeon, and at 12-45 emerged once more on the hillside above Bradwell. And whilst we sat at supper in

the Bull's Head, the light came broadening out over Bradwell Edge and the morning birds began to sing.

About a week later, the series of passages that we discovered below the Dungeon were further explored by Mr. Maurice Shaw, of Bradwell, and Mr. James Porter, of Owens College, who were able to verify the conjecture that these communicated with the big chamber known to exist near Bradwell Dale. After crawling along many difficult tunnels and wading through several lakelets, they reached a point where they could hear the Bradwell water running out from its subterranean channel into the open air. They also heard a cart jolting along close by on the highway; yet the passages were too low or the water too high for them to crawl through. They returned afterwards with three other men from Owens College, and attained a lofty chamber bountifully adorned with curtains of stalactite, the finest cavern in the Bagshawe series, they judged it, and by way of a branching passage they got to the Bradwell water, but could not squeeze through to the exit, which, however, could not have been far away.

XXVI.

CAVE-WORK AS A SPORT.

THE Bagshawe was the last of the great Derbyshire caverns that we explored. Doubtless the enormous thickness of carboniferous limestone that underlies a large area of the Peak contains other cavities and water channels that equal any of these in extent, though they may never be revealed to living eye; but the numerous other caves that have been explored are of quite inferior interest. I may conclude with some observations on the general aspects of cave exploration, whether we call it speleology and regard it in the light of a science, or whether we follow it merely as a novel and exciting sport. In these pages the scientific aspect of cave-exploration has not been obtruded, but it is obvious that such underground work can furnish materials for increase of knowledge to the geologist, the petrologist, the mineralogist, the hydrographer, and the palæontologist, with a great many other scientists of equally sonorous designations. But, regarded as a sport, in the way that even the professed scientist must regard it more or less, what is to be said for it?

After my lugubrious experience in our first descent into Elden Hole, I was near making a resolution never again to venture inside a cavern or pot-hole. But the men who had shared the risks of our adventure, yet had been cheated of their hopes of going down, required the services of me and my fellow-sufferer for a more elaborate exploration, whence all the dangers and most of the discomforts were to be eliminated. It would have been churlish and ungrateful not to volunteer, but the fatal result was that we were suddenly turned into ardent cave-explorers, and ever since have seized every opportunity of going down into the earth's secret places. Whence, then, the charms of this uncleanly and topsy-turvy pastime?

First, of course, must be put the beauty and sublimity that lie concealed in the subterranean darkness. There is a tremendous suggestion of latent power about these rifts and cavities in the solid structure of the earth. A stream on the surface of the ground is a beautiful, or may be a grand object; but put the same stream in a deep cavern, or a stream that is not half so big and powerful, and the impression it makes on the senses of those who see and hear it, is incomparably greater. A little waterfall, enclosed by the resonant, bell-shaped walls of a cave, awakens thunderous echoes that rival the noise of a great cataract; the far-heard muttering, the terrible crescendo as we draw nearer and nearer, and the deafening and soul-shaking voice of the imminent torrent plunging into dark abysms, is a sound never to be forgotten, a sound to haunt bad dreams.

But not merely these gloomy streams, with their black swallet-holes, strange disappearances, and stormy descents, are enveloped in a mystery that fascinates while it awes; it is the same with all things underground. Every cave is a cave of illusions. Mere size and height measured in so many feet are as nothing compared with the vastness of the impression that it makes with its hidden distances, impenetrable shadows, and the vagueness of its fugitive outlines. Ordinary means of illumination reveal only the area immediately around one, leaving the remoter spaces massed in deeper shadow. The most powerful searchlight cannot utterly dethrone the majesty of darkness. Then there is the zest of possible discovery. At any moment you may break into some treasure chamber of natural beauty never yet disclosed to human eye; you are ever on the tip-toe of expectation. And there is an immense difference between the public shows of a cave that has been open and accessible for years, a crust of dirt and soot covering every inch of the dulled stalactites, and the pure, unsullied beauty of these crystallisations fresh from Nature's laboratory.

But a sport is a sport independently of æsthetic and scientific attractions. All it requires is some object to pursue, some definite aim for strenuous activity, co-operative or competitive. And this brings me to the attraction that may well be the keenest of all to some minds, namely, the danger. Not that cave exploration is to be ranked among the pastimes that involve a certain percentage of disasters; I do not think there has ever been a fatal accident placed to its account. Yet cave-work does belong to that masculine class of sports, of which mountaineering and rock-climbing are the type, which incessantly bring their followers into the presence of danger. Their aim is neither to court nor to avoid, but, if I may so put it, to annihilate danger. Skill gotten of experience, strength of muscle, and presence of mind are the means of accomplishing this, and the cultivation of these virtues is a not unworthy end of any sport. I should not, however, put cave-work on the same level with crag-climbing, although in Derbyshire, curiously, many of our finest rock-climbs are under-ground. The perils of rock-climbing are frank and open, those of cave-work are of an insidious and more intimidating kind. Climbing is the most exhilarating of sports, the joys of cave wandering are won in defiance of all that seems most gloomy and depressing. Nor as an exercise is it equal to climbing in the open air. The exertion is often far more arduous; there are few kinds of physical discipline more trying than to crawl on your stomach over sharp rocks, with no space to lift your head for hundreds of yards perhaps, and one arm cramped with holding a flaring candle out in front, which keeps burning your fingers. Then there is heavy apparatus to carry up and down tunnels and funnels of the most inconvenient shape—exhausting work, and all without the stimulus that makes hard work a benefit and a pleasure, abundance of oxygen. Certainly, cave-exploration is not as good a game as climbing, but, within the limits I suggest, is there another to equal it?

The Derbyshire caverns are surpassed in brilliance by the stalactite caves of Cheddar, by the many-hued masses of incrustation in Lamb's Lair, and the snowy terraces and rich emblazonries of Swildon's Hole and other caves in Somerset. They can show nothing so grimly impressive as Gaping Ghyll and Helln Pot, in Yorkshire. But in variety of configuration, and, accordingly, in the variety of sport they offer, our caves are equal to any. Though a dry cave, the Blue John is remarkable for its diversity of interest. The Bagshawe Cavern is of a totally different character; but in spite of its generally horizontal direction, its lakes and streams and the irregular conformation of its ramifying passages show the same interesting diversity. The Speedwell is another type of cavern altogether. Its unmeasured roof, more awe-inspiring than its dark and gloomy pit, still offers a virgin climb to intrepid adventurers; and its inundated levels open into natural canals and deserted water-channels that enfold romantic possibilities of discovery. Peak Cavern, in spite of M. Martel's disparagement, is still interesting. Its strange configuration combines a number of features that are not often found together, and the thorough-going explorer must be prepared to descend swallets, to climb fissures of unknown height, and to paddle his skiff into most uncanny waterways. Of caves that are entered at the top instead of the lower exit, there are Elden Hole, Bull Pit, Owl Hole, Gautries Hill Pit, and many more of the perpendicular kind; and Giant's Hole, Manifold at Perryfoot, and countless others that open along horizontal fissures. These we have explored as far as might be done without excavation. But it is to be remembered that work with pick and shovel may at any time disclose a new range of possibilities. In Somerset, a friend of mine, by opening a swallet similar to those near Perryfoot, discovered a cave that extended 2,000 feet and to a depth of 600 feet below the surface. Probably there are unknown caves in Derbyshire of equal or greater extent, and accident or persevering exploration may some day lead to their discovery. The streams between Perryfoot and Giant's Hole run away into solid rock that offers little opportunity for excavation. Larger streams, small rivers indeed, in different parts of Derbyshire, slip into the earth, and run underground for several miles. These may, perhaps, afford to the cave-explorer of the future finer sport than any we have met with hitherto.

FINIS.

THE BAGSHAWE C

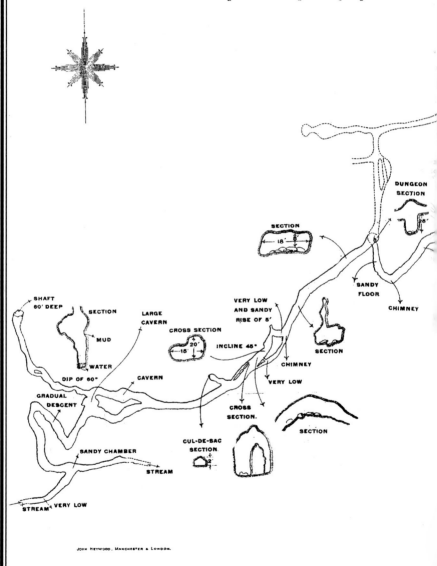